DOUBLE DUTY

DOUBLE DUTY

The Parents' Guide to Raising Twins,
from Pregnancy Through the School Years

CHRISTINA BAGLIVI TINGLOF

CB

CONTEMPORARY BOOKS

Library of Congress Cataloging-in-Publication Data

Tinglof, Christina Baglivi.
    Double duty : the parents' guide to raising twins, from pregnancy through
the school years / Christina Baglivi Tinglof.
       p.   cm.
    Includes index.
    ISBN 0-8092-3019-4
    1. Twins   2. Child rearing.   3. Infants—Care.   4. Pregnancy.
I. Title.
HQ777.35.T56   1998
649'.1—dc21   97-38764
                                                           CIP

Cover design by Todd Petersen
Cover photograph copyright © Anne Nielsen/Tony Stone Images
Interior design by Mary Lockwood
Interior art by Precision Graphics

Published by Contemporary Books
A division of NTC/Contemporary Publishing Group, Inc.
4255 West Touhy Avenue, Lincolnwood (Chicago), Illinois 60646-1975 U.S.A.
Manufactured in the United States of America
International Standard Book Number: 0-8092-3019-4

99 00 01 02 03 04 MV 18 17 16 15 14 13 12 11 10 9 8 7 6 5 4 3 2

To my beautiful sons, Joseph and Michael; and in loving memory of their grandmother, Rosemarie Marasco Baglivi, who would have spoiled them rotten

Contents

Foreword

It is hard to describe the thrill my patient and I feel when I diagnose a twin pregnancy. The scene is typically played out in much the same way every time: An otherwise healthy mother-to-be comes into my office anxious and nervous, feeling that "something is just not right" with her pregnancy. Her abdomen is too big; she feels a strange movement or strong abdominal pressure; or a friend has told her that something is wrong. After I calm and reassure her, off we go to the ultrasound room to check things out. Keeping my suspicions to myself, I take a good long look, then once I am convinced, I show my patient her double miracle on the ultrasound screen. She usually sits there in absolute shock, while I get a good chuckle out of this universal response.

With advanced fertility techniques in practice today, doctors are seeing a large increase in the number of multiple births. Twenty years ago it was rare to diagnose a twin pregnancy, but today I am usually caring for two or three sets of twin pregnancies at the same time!

After Mom and Dad survive the shock of knowing that they are going to double their pleasure as well as their expenses (preschool, clothing, medical fees, college, and so on), I sit them down to discuss the management of this very special pregnancy. Each physician has his or her own level of comfort and established management protocol for a multiple pregnancy. Twin pregnancies are unique and need to be handled with extra vigilance. Many issues come up with two babies that usually do not present themselves as problems with a singleton pregnancy. Families of twins need more explanations and greater attention to very fine details to maximize the chances for a good outcome. A twin pregnancy entails more prenatal office visits, additional ultrasounds, and a higher index of suspicion for problems. In addition, patients often need to modify their expectations—they may have to make major lifestyle changes during pregnancy, or they may end up hospitalized for a large percentage of pregnancy. Despite all this, twin pregnancies today often have happy and beautiful outcomes for both the babies and their families. Taking care of patients expecting twins is a privilege as well as a challenge. And when two beautiful healthy babies are delivered, it is thrilling for everyone involved.

This book, *Double Duty: The Parents' Guide to Raising Twins, from Pregnancy Through the School Years* by Christina Baglivi Tinglof, deals with all the important aspects of raising twins, from pregnancy through early childhood. Clearly, there is no better authority than someone who has lived through the triumphs and the tribulations herself as Christina has. *Double Duty* provides the answers to the questions that only other parents of twins can answer. As an obstetrician-gynecologist, I live through the first nine months with my patients and provide technical advice and all the support I can. *Double Duty* supplies the nitty-gritty, real-life advice. The book covers issues from varying points of view, offering nonjudgmental advice and different perspectives on the many issues involved in raising twins. By reviewing a variety of opinions, parents may selectively gather information that is helpful for their particular lifestyle or situation. The book gives a concise, hands-on collection of insight and shared experiences that would be extremely helpful to expectant families or those currently facing the challenging day-to-day encounters with twins.

I commend Christina for her two beautiful babies and for finding the time and the determination to write this book.

Kim Bader, M.D.

Acknowledgments

My deepest thanks to all for their support and hard work during the past year.

First and foremost, I'd like to thank my agent, Betsy Amster, for her enthusiasm, support, and guidance. Many thanks to my editor, Kara Leverte, for transforming my manuscript to a finished book. To Dr. Kim Bader for penning the book's foreword and for her helpful suggestions for the pregnancy chapter. To Christina Elston for her great matchmaking abilities. To MaryElla Donleavy and Joanna Marasco for their help in researching the book.

To the many parents of twins and twins themselves who openly shared their thoughts, experiences, and insights on twinship, including Elizabeth Near, Cynthia Guinnip, Patty Watson-Wood, Andrea Lussier, Kathleen Riggs, Ann Wilson, Linda Sweeney, Janice Smith, David Smith, Brian Smith, Kathy Mazer, Buddy and Dawn Rowe, David Story, Mae Young, Marianne Critchley Schobel, Bradley Kennedy, Irene Chavez, Nannette Chavez, Yvette Chavez, Tim Meador, Sherrie Butler, William and Verna Valley, John and Brenda Baker, Don and Paula Alanzo, and Karen and Barry Vogel.

To Claire Spelta, Mary Hagen, Christie Lear, and Laurie Viera for all their help during the months following the birth of my sons, as well as their continued loving support (not to mention free baby-sitting services). And to Gina Ferrara Bates, my sounding board, for her unique perspective on child rearing.

And finally, to my husband, Kevin — a doting and patient father, a caring husband, a wise soul, and my best friend.

Introduction

Like the thousands of other couples before us, my husband, Kevin, and I learned about the impending arrival of our double bundle of joy while in the ultrasound room. Just six weeks into my pregnancy, I lay on the examining table with Kevin by my side, craning my neck to see the video screen. (A high level of HCG in my blood prompted the early visit and subsequent diagnosis.) Barely visible to our untrained eyes, two tiny hearts blinked in unison against a dark backdrop, flickering like interstellar fireflies. My doctor's suspicions were confirmed—we were expecting twins.

Our first reactions were similar to the ones you probably felt when you learned the news: disbelief, excitement, and, of course, fear. Yet here it is a mere two years after the birth of our fraternal boys, Joseph and Michael, and life feels remarkably natural and normal, as if every mother gives birth to twins.

Like you, we were worried about the pregnancy and whether the babies would be born healthy. I had read that twins often show up prematurely (three weeks on average) and that it was extremely important that I take exceptional care of myself to ensure a happy outcome. My efforts (and prayers) paid off—I carried my sons to term. Joseph weighed in at 6 pounds, 8 ounces; Michael at 6 pounds, 12 ounces.

Like most things in life, having twins has its ups and downs. You are *doubly blessed*. There is nothing more magical than two smiling faces greeting you first thing in the morning, or two warm bundles to snuggle up to in the evening. It's truly a miracle. Families who want only two children get their childbearing over with sooner—with twins, you have an instant family. The twins themselves share a special bond that begins in infancy, and they become confidantes for life.

Yet there are drawbacks. Having twins can be exhausting. Someone *always* wants and needs you. Parents of twins often feel guilty about never having enough time to devote to one child or the other. And the twins themselves are raised differently than a singleton simply because they were born as a pair. Psychologists theorize that it is normal for every infant to begin life completely self-centered, monopolizing his mother's attention. This, they say, is how the baby's ego is formed. Twins, on the other hand, are born into a life of competition. A twin must always wait her turn. But when all is said and done, would I trade places with a mother of a singleton? Not on your life! I have *four* cheeks to kiss, not just two.

In my book, *Double Duty: The Parents' Guide to Raising Twins, from Pregnancy Through the School Years,* parents expecting twins get practical strategies for coping with the challenges that lie ahead (and believe me, there will be plenty). With a wealth of tips from more than 20 families with twins who lived to tell about it (as well as some twins themselves), the book covers pregnancy through the first days of school. Every type of family is included: families with stay-at-home parents, families with both parents working, families with newborn twins, toddler twins, school-age twins, identical twins, fraternal twins—you name it. Through trial and error, these resourceful mothers and fathers have learned to successfully manage their often hectic lives and now share their insights with you.

Double Duty also includes Top Five Lists, a quick reference to the most popular ways of handling your duo from the "Top Five Birthday Party No-Nos" to the "Top Five Twin Gadgets," as well as Developmental Milestones—many unique to twins—so that you know what to expect both physically and emotionally from your doppelgängers in the coming months. For instance, don't expect your babies to start actively interacting until they've reached their first birthday. But once they've hit that marker, their twinness will blossom and become fascinating to observe. Twins will temporarily choose roles in their relationship—one will become the leader, the other, the follower. But several months later, they often reverse positions (just to keep you on your toes).

Mostly, though, *Double Duty* shares strategies about the day-to-day circumstances that new parents of twins face, from how to nurse two babies at once to getting twins on the same schedule. Whether you're concerned about giving each baby enough individualized attention or deciding whether to put them in the same class in school, *Double Duty* has the answer. Let it be your guide to life with multiples. Happy trails!

DOUBLE DUTY

•1•

So You're Having Twins

Parents of twins hear all sorts of odd questions and misinformed comments about twinning from friends and family (and even strangers), such as "Are they paternal twins?" and "I thought all same-sex twins were identical!" High school science class covered the basics, but most folks have forgotten why and how this phenomenon happens. What follows in the next few pages is a crash course in Biology 101 so that you may go out and reeducate the world on the miracle of twinning. Now, class, pay attention . . .

Just the Stats, Ma'am

A staggering 95 percent of all multiples are twins, and more than 125 million sets roam the world today. The number of multiples, particularly twins, has been on the rise since the early 1980s, when doctors first learned how to make women superovulate, or release multiple eggs in one cycle. In 1994 (the most recent year for which statistics are available), the U.S. reported more than 96,000 twin births, compared with approximately 66,000 in 1980 and 54,000 in 1973. During the 1980s, twins occurred in one of every 80 to 90 births, while today twinning happens in every 40 to 45. And while the number of dizygotic (or fraternal) twins has varied through the years, the number of monozygotic (or identical) twins has remained constant, about 4 per 1,000 births.

Why the Increase?

The explosion of twinning is really an increase in the number of fraternal twins. (Identical twins are considered a random fluke of nature; therefore, the numbers have remained fairly constant over the years.) The increase is due to a number of biological, medical, and environmental factors.

FERTILITY DRUGS

During the late 1970s, fertility drugs became widely available to couples who had problems conceiving. Clomiphene citrate (Clomid), the most common of all fertility drugs, helps the woman's body ripen eggs in the ovaries and release them at the time of ovulation. A woman who takes clomiphene citrate increases her chances of twinning by 10 percent (although some doctors say the percentage is much higher). A woman's likelihood of a multiple birth rises even further if she takes a more potent fertility drug called Pergonal. Its use often results in the birth of quadruplets and even quintuplets.

AGE

A woman who delays childbearing until after the age of 30 is also at a greater risk of twinning. As a woman gets older, she produces higher levels of gonadotropins (peaking between the ages of 35 and 39), hormones that stimulate the ovaries to release more eggs. One of these hormones is the follicle-stimulating hormone (FSH) that is responsible for ovulation. A 35- to 40-year-old woman is three times more likely to have twins than a woman who is 20 to 24 years old.

BIRTH CONTROL PILLS

A woman who gets pregnant shortly after the cessation of birth control pills has a greater chance of conceiving twins as well, although the results have been found to be inconclusive in some studies.

IN-VITRO FERTILIZATION

Of all the high-tech procedures around these days to help infertile couples conceive, in-vitro fertilization (IVF) is the most common. First introduced to the United States in 1980, IVF involves removing eggs from the mother, fertilizing them in the laboratory, and then implanting the embryos back in her uterus. Several are implanted at once to increase the likelihood of success. Often the procedure is so successful that two, three, or more embryos prove to be viable (about 25 percent of IVF pregnancies produce twins).

INHERITED TRAIT

Yes, twins do run in families, but only fraternal twins (not identical) and only through the female bloodline. So if your mom is a fraternal twin, or has a set in her family, that could explain why you are expecting twins.

WOMEN WHO ALREADY HAVE HAD CHILDREN

Due to hormonal changes, the more children a woman has the more likely she will conceive twins with each successive birth.

WOMEN WHO ALREADY HAVE HAD FRATERNAL TWINS

Yes, lightning can strike the same place twice—a woman who has already given birth to fraternal twins doubles her chances of repeating it again with her next pregnancy.

RACE

African races have the highest incidence of twinning (about 20 percent more likely than Caucasian women), followed by Europeans, then Mexicans. Asians have the lowest incidence.

BODY TYPE

If a woman is tall and heavy, her chances of having twins increase.

Twin Types

There are only two types of twins—fraternal, who share 50 percent of their genes (at best), and identical, who share 100 percent. Fertilization determines twin type.

FRATERNAL

The most common type of twins, fraternal (or dizygotic), occurs when two separate eggs are fertilized by two separate sperm. Fraternal twins have different DNA (at most they share only 50 percent) and often don't look anything alike. They're simply wombmates, two siblings sharing the same space for nine months.

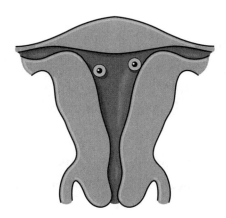

Fraternal twins are formed when two eggs are fertilized by two sperm.

IDENTICAL

An anomaly in nature, identical (or monozygotic) twins happen when one egg, fertilized by one sperm, splits into two. Identical twins share the exact same DNA and therefore are always the same sex and look exactly alike. Identical twins account for only 30 percent of twinship. Twenty-five percent of identicals are *mirror twins*—that is, many facial traits like dental patterns and birthmarks appear on opposite sides of each twin's face.

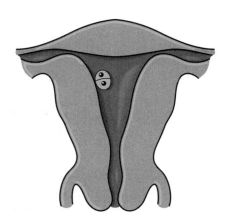

Identical twins are formed when one fertilized egg splits into two embryos.

Determining Twin Type

Unless your twins are a boy and a girl, determining twin type can be tricky, especially immediately following their birth. (Don't all newborns look alike?) As the twins get older, varying physical appearance or growing similarities will shed some light as to their type, yet many fraternal twins look remarkably alike. The only reliable method to determine twin type is DNA testing or blood testing of the umbilical cord — both costly procedures.

Myths or Miracles?

Think you've got this biology stuff figured out? Let's find out: answer *true* or *false* to the following twin tales.

Twins occur every other generation.

False Just an old wives' tale. Twinning can happen in any generation.

Most twins don't look alike.

True *Only one third of all twins are identical. Fraternal twins are simply siblings who share a common birthday.*

If there's only one placenta, the twins must be identical.

False It ain't necessarily so. Sometimes two separate placentas fuse together, giving the appearance of one. The only true way to tell if twins are fraternal or identical (unless they are boy and girl) is through testing.

If you're an identical twin, your chances of having twins will increase dramatically.

False Identical twins are nature's toss of the dice and aren't passed down from family to family. Only fraternal twins run in families.

Now It's Your Turn

Armed with these exciting twin facts and figures, go out into the world and dispel the myths! As a newly chosen "multiple missionary," it's your turn to educate the world (or at least your family and friends) about twinning.

•2•

Fifty Pounds and Still Gaining— Coping with Pregnancy

I was wearing maternity clothes by Week 10. By my seventh month people kept asking me when I was due. I felt like a whale and counted the days until my due date. They say twins come early, but not my sons—the doctors had to induce me. But Anthony and Julian were big, healthy babies, weighing more than 6 pounds each!

Forget the old saying, "You're eating for two." You're eating for *three*— a sometimes awesome task. And while most women can expect to gain 25 to 30 pounds with a singleton pregnancy, your doctor probably told you that you should put on close to 60. Gaining extra weight is just one of many concerns for a woman carrying twins. Twin pregnancies at any age are considered *high risk*, a term that often sounds worse than it is. Remember, most mothers-to-be breeze through a twin pregnancy with nary a complaint. Unfortunately, others are confined to bed early on with complications stemming from an engineering glitch in the human body—women were designed to carry only one fetus at a time. You can ease your anxieties and give yourself a sense of control over your pregnancy by reading everything you can on multiple births, and following the advice of your physician. This chapter focuses on your pregnancy and what you can do to help bring healthy babies into the world.

When she came home from her ultrasound appointment, she said, "There are two." I couldn't understand what she was saying at first. So I said, "What do you mean two? Two what?"

Prenatal Care

You dream that the birth of your children will be a day of joy with few, if any, complications. Yet you can't ignore that little voice in the back of your head that keeps whispering, "What if there's a problem?" While no one can guarantee smooth sailing, good prenatal care— including a diet high in protein—provides the best chance for a healthy outcome for both you and your babies. Keep all scheduled doctor's appointments and slow down your lifestyle according to her recommendations.

Choosing a Doctor

Your relationship with your obstetrician is an important one. Since you'll be asking her many questions throughout your pregnancy and deciding on a host of important issues, including which prenatal tests to undergo, you should feel a strong sense of trust and comfort. One way to find a qualified obstetrician is to call your local hospital's doctor referral service or local Mothers of Twins Club (MOTC) for a list of recommendations.

Try to choose a health care provider with experience in multiple births and high-risk pregnancies. You and your doctor should have similar views on pregnancy and birthing as well. Does she routinely perform cesarean sections on all multiple births, while you feel strongly about trying to have a vaginal birth? What treatment does she prescribe if problems do arise? Many tests and techniques involving a multiple birth vary widely and some are considered controversial. Do you agree with your physician's point of view? If not, you might want to interview another obstetrician.

Hospital Affiliation

Even if you take excellent care of yourself and follow your doctor's advice to the letter, twins sometimes show up early (three weeks on average), and in some cases very early, requiring an extended stay in a neonatal intensive care unit (NICU). When searching for your obstetrician, try to find one affiliated with a Level III hospital with a topnotch NICU. Otherwise, if your newborns do need to be placed in the NICU and your hospital doesn't have one, your babies will be transported to a better-equipped facility, away from you.

Chances are that your twins won't need the NICU, but preparing yourself mentally by visiting the unit, talking with the NICU staff, and familiarizing yourself with the various machines and their functions while on your hospital tour is a good idea. It will help ease the possible emotional strain on you and your family if your babies are born prematurely and need the assistance of the NICU.

BUT I DON'T FEEL HIGH RISK

Even if you feel great throughout your pregnancy, multiple births are more likely to run into medical complications than singleton deliveries and therefore earn the title *high risk*. For this reason, moms carrying twins are monitored more closely than those carrying singletons. You'll visit your doctor more often—usually every three weeks until Week 20, every two weeks until Week 30, then weekly thereafter—and undergo more prenatal tests.

PRENATAL TESTS

Even healthy twin pregnancies require more poking and prodding than singleton pregnancies. However, some doctors prescribe more tests than others. Following is a brief list of standard tests that you'll encounter. Each has its benefits as well as its risks and should be discussed at length with your obstetrician.

Ultrasound

What? One of the most widely used prenatal tests, ultrasound (or sonogram) uses high-frequency sound waves, takes only a few minutes to perform, and is relatively painless. The doctor or technician rubs a thin layer of jelly across a pregnant woman's lower abdomen, then moves a transducer across the area. As the sound waves bounce off the baby's bones and tissues, an image appears on a television screen.

Why? To confirm a multiple pregnancy. Ultrasound is also useful for detecting malformations like spina bifida, or abnormalities of the brain, heart, liver, or kidneys. Later in pregnancy it's used to show the position of the baby (or babies) and to monitor fetal growth and weight. It also accurately determines gestational age. Ultrasound can sometimes determine fetal sex, though not with complete reliability.

When and How Often? Ultrasounds are routinely given once between Weeks 16 and 18. For women expecting twins, however, the doctor may order a series of ultrasounds every few weeks, depending on the progress of the mother.

Pros and Cons. Considered a safe procedure since no harmful X rays are involved, ultrasound is one of the least invasive prenatal procedures. Parents' concerns about the health of their babies are immediately put at ease without lengthy waits for lab results. In recent years some researchers have voiced concern over possible harm to the fetus, but evidence to prove this claim has never been established. The benefits in safely accessing the fetuses in a multiple pregnancy make ultrasound a commonly recommended test.

Amniocentesis

What? Amniocentesis, generally considered a safe procedure, involves removing a small amount of amniotic fluid from the amniotic sac, the bag of water that surrounds the fetus (or fetuses). With the help of ultrasound, a safe insertion spot away from the fetus is established and then a needle is inserted through the abdominal wall and into the uterus. The procedure takes about 30 minutes to perform and the patient may feel a small amount of discomfort.

Why? Amniocentesis is used most often to detect chromosomal abnormalities like Down's syndrome in fetuses of patients over the age of 35. The test can also recognize autosomal recessive diseases like sickle-cell anemia, cystic fibrosis, and Tay-Sachs. It can confirm the baby's sex and therefore is important for a family with a history of sex-linked diseases like hemophilia. During the third trimester, amniocentesis is invaluable in determining the maturity of a baby's lungs if premature delivery seems inevitable.

When and How Often? Although amniocentesis is usually performed once between Weeks 16 and 20, the clinician may order a second toward the end of the pregnancy to establish the maturity of the baby's lungs when a woman is experiencing problems in her pregnancy and premature delivery is inevitable.

Pros and Cons. Waiting the required week or two for amniocentesis results can put a strain on any couple, but the peace of mind that follows after hearing that the test results are negative helps families relax and enjoy the remaining months of pregnancy. On the other hand, a major downfall to amniocentesis is the relatively late time in the pregnancy it is performed, making it difficult for those waiting for genetic analysis and who may be faced with the decision of whether or not to abort. Furthermore, amniocentesis is more difficult to perform on a twin pregnancy since both sacs must be evaluated and on occasion the second sac can't be located; it's very expensive (about $1,000 for each test); and there's a small chance of spontaneous abortion (less than .05 percent, but higher in women with multiples) or infection.

Chorionic Villus Sampling (cvs)

What? Chorionic villus sampling (cvs) is relatively new in the medical community. With the aid of ultrasound, a catheter (thin tube) is inserted into a woman's cervix and a small amount of placenta cells are extracted and then cultured in a laboratory.

Why? The test can detect chromosomal abnormalities such as Down's syndrome.

When and How Often? Cvs is usually performed once between Weeks 10 and 12.

Pros and Cons. Since cvs can be performed early in pregnancy, some couples choose it over amniocentesis. Primary results are available within 48 hours (compared to the standard two weeks for amniocentesis results). The downside of cvs, though, is its higher risk of spontaneous abortion (approximately 1 percent) as well as the possibility of fetal limb defects (documented in patients who had the procedure done prior to 10.5 weeks).

Maternal Serum Alpha-Fetoprotein Test (MSAFP)

What? MSAFP is a painless blood test used to measure a specific protein made by the baby (or babies) and circulated in the mother's bloodstream.

Why? The test offers a noninvasive way to analyze the health of the fetus. High levels of alpha-fetoprotein (AFP) can indicate a neural tube defect such as spina bifida, or it can simply mean a multiple pregnancy. Low levels may indicate Down's syndrome.

When and How Often? The test is usually given once between Weeks 16 and 20.

Pros and Cons. Considered by some to be a controversial test, MSAFP's biggest drawback is its sometimes inaccurate results in the form of false positives and false negatives. Women with false positive results require additional tests, worrying them needlessly. If levels of AFP are low, an expensive amniocentesis may be prescribed to confirm or deny the existence of Down's syndrome. If levels are high, parents might jump to the wrong conclusion that their baby has a neural tube defect, only to discover later through ultrasound that the blood results simply mean that the couple is expecting twins. The blood test is not necessary for women who already plan on having an amniocentesis.

Nonstress Test

What? External ultrasound monitors are attached to a woman's abdomen in order to monitor the fetal heartbeat. The results are printed out and then evaluated by a physician.

Why? The test is usually used during the third trimester to assess fetal well-being due to stress from maternal high blood pressure, the overcrowding in the uterus due to multiples, or other medical problems associated with a high-risk pregnancy.

When and How Often? When deemed necessary by a physician, the nonstress test is administered weekly during the last trimester, usually after Week 30, and sometimes twice weekly after Week 32.

Pros and Cons. A painless and safe procedure. There are no immediate drawbacks, except that it can take up to an hour to perform and is expensive.

POSSIBLE MATERNAL COMPLICATIONS

The following are complications that *may* happen during pregnancy. Chances are they *won't* happen. Statistically, mothers carrying twins do experience more problems, but keep in mind that statistics are only as reliable as the population they study. Since most research is carried out at major medical centers, many participants are already deemed high risk. The odds are that if you take good care of yourself by eating right, getting enough rest, and visiting your doctor regularly, your babies will be born big and healthy.

Bleeding

Spotting is common in early pregnancy and seems more serious than it usually is. While some women bleed on and off throughout their entire pregnancies without any ill effects to their babies, a woman experiencing vaginal bleeding should err on the side of caution and notify her physician. In some cases, bleeding in the early months could mean an impending miscarriage of one or both babies or ectopic pregnancy. In late pregnancy, bleeding may mean that the placenta is separating from the uterus (abruptio placentae), or partially covering the cervix (placenta previa), both requiring immediate medical attention. Bleeding during sexual intercourse may indicate a cervical polyp or vaginal infection.

Edema

As the babies grow and crowd the pelvis, circulation slows, causing a swelling of the ankles and hands. When this happens, it's best to lie down with your feet propped up. If your hands continue to swell and your face becomes swollen, it could be a sign of toxemia and should be reported to the doctor immediately.

Preeclampsia

Preeclampsia, or toxemia, is characterized by extremely high blood pressure. The cause is not known, but it affects about 5 percent of all pregnancies, and nearly 20 percent of twin pregnancies. Careful screening of blood pressure, monitoring swelling of the hands and feet, and testing for protein in the urine, especially during the third trimester, are the best ways to assess whether a woman is at risk for developing preeclampsia. Other signs include headaches and epigastric pain. If preeclampsia goes unchecked and untreated, it can develop into eclampsia, a dangerous condition for both mothers and babies.

Gestational Diabetes

Gestational diabetes develops during the latter half of the second trimester or early part of the third trimester and then can resolve itself after the babies are born. The condition occurs when there is a change in a pregnant woman's glucose metabolism as her body puts more demands on the pancreas to produce more insulin, resulting in the insulin resistance. If a woman develops gestational diabetes, her chances of preeclampsia increase. She may also experience complications during delivery and might be at risk for developing adult-onset diabetes later in life. A glucose tolerance test is given during the second or third trimester to screen for the disease. Women with borderline gestational diabetes are put on a strict diet high in protein and low in carbohydrates, while women who develop the condition require insulin during the remainder of their pregnancies.

Anemia

Anemia occurs when a woman's body isn't producing enough red blood cells to transport oxygen to her babies. As the babies grow, they deplete the mother's iron supply. In severe cases, anemia can cause preterm labor. A diet rich in iron and folic acid may not be enough to prevent anemia, and often a doctor will prescribe additional iron supplements—especially if a woman develops a mild dilutional anemia after 28 weeks of pregnancy, as most do.

Cesarean Delivery

Nearly 50 percent of twins are delivered by cesarean, due in large part to added complications associated with multiple delivery and to a medical community that shies away from breech (fetus in feet-first position) or transverse (fetus in horizontal position) deliveries. In about half of all twin pregnancies, both babies will be in the vertex (head-down) position—but in the remaining 50 percent, one or both babies are either in the breech or transverse position. Sometimes after the first baby is born vaginally, the physician can manually massage the mother's abdomen to turn the second baby into the head-down position, thereby avoiding a cesarean delivery.

POSSIBLE FETAL COMPLICATIONS

Once again, it's important to remember that most babies do just fine. The following fetal complications are listed merely to keep you informed about some things that *may* happen.

Twin Transfusion Syndrome

Twin transfusion syndrome occurs only with identical twins who share a common placenta with an abnormal vascular problem. One twin receives too much blood and nutrition while the other doesn't receive enough. Both babies suffer—the donor is often born underweight and anemic, while the recipient can experience jaundice, respiratory problems, or even heart failure. Ultrasound can often detect the problem, and medical intervention has been successful.

Placenta Previa

A condition where the placenta covers part or all of the cervix, placenta previa is twice as likely to happen to a mother expecting twins as a woman carrying a singleton. Usually, the only symptom of this condition is slight bleeding without any discomfort. After the mother's and babies' conditions have been assessed through ultrasound, bed rest is usually recommended. If placenta previa occurs during the early months of pregnancy, the placenta often grows up and away from the cervix, but if it occurs later in pregnancy, and the condition does not correct itself, cesarean delivery is required.

Vanishing Twin Syndrome

Sometimes during the early part of pregnancy, one baby stops developing and is either miscarried or absorbed into the mother's body while the other baby continues to thrive. Often the mother isn't aware she is carrying twins until she experiences spotting and verifies this phenomenon through an ultrasound assessment.

Preterm Labor

The number one problem of moms expecting twins, preterm labor happens when the babies decide to show up between Weeks 20 and 36 of gestation. Nearly 50 percent of mothers carrying twins experience preterm labor. The cause is not clear, but it's speculated that poor weight gain through inadequate nutrition, an infection in the mother, a history of prior preterm labor, preeclampsia, smoking, maternal age (under 16 or over 35), benign uterine tumors, or simply overcrowding in the uterus due to multiple fetuses could contribute to preterm labor. In some cases, preterm labor can be stopped through drug therapy.

> *I didn't know that I was going into labor. I had noticed a bit of spotting and so I was concerned. I called the doctor and he said, "Why don't you come in so we can check it?" Once we got there, I was already in labor, and it was too late. They tried to put me on medication to hold off labor, but that didn't work. (Marianne delivered at 31 weeks. Her sons weighed a little more than 3 pounds each and spent about 6 weeks in* NICU.)

PRETERM WARNING SIGNS

Labor can come on quickly. If you experience any of the symptoms listed below, don't hesitate to call your doctor immediately.

- The onset of contractions (five or more per hour, lasting 40 seconds or longer), not to be confused with normal Braxton-Hicks contractions (lasting 20 to 30 seconds; usually irregular; and disappearing after an hour, a change of position, or drinking lots of fluids)

- Low, dull backache, menstrual-like cramps, or extreme pelvic pressure

- Release of amniotic fluid or mucus plug, or vaginal bleeding

- Diarrhea or strong intestinal discomfort

- The strong feeling that something is wrong

> I felt really funny that day. I had a few of the symptoms that I had read about—an upset stomach, a little bit of cramping, and just an uneasy feeling. Then I started spotting, so I called the doctor and she said come on into the hospital. They hooked me up to a monitor and I was having contractions. (Sherrie went into preterm labor at 25 weeks, but the doctors were able to stop it in time through medication. She then went on to carry her twins to 35½ weeks.)

LOW BIRTH WEIGHT

While premature infants often suffer from low birth weight, prematurity and low birth weight should not be confused. Low birth weight babies, defined as infants weighing less than 5 pounds, 8 ounces at term (2,500 grams), are at a higher risk of developing problems during infancy. A mother's best chance of delivering plump, healthy babies is to see her doctor regularly; abstain from tobacco, alcohol, and other drugs; and eat a high-calorie diet rich in protein and complex carbohydrates.

INTERVENTIONS TO HELP PROLONG PREGNANCY

Many of the complications women experience in a multiple pregnancy can be alleviated with proper and timely medical intervention. If a mother expecting twins goes into labor before 36 weeks, often her doctor will try to stop it with complete bed rest or prescription medication.

Bed Rest

Some doctors still routinely prescribe several weeks of bed rest to prevent premature delivery during a woman's last trimester if she is expecting twins. The most common (and the most controversial) medical intervention, bed rest can mean anything from round-the-clock confinement to just a few hours a day, in a semi-reclining position or lying down completely. With bed rest, some physicians reason, the weight and stress of carrying more than one fetus are taken off the cervix. In addition, they say, more nutrients will reach the babies through the placenta because the mother's blood flow increases. But bed rest has its critics. Some research indicates that bed rest doesn't do anything to prevent premature delivery and that complete bed rest will heighten a woman's chances of a blood clot and may actually increase her blood pressure, which often leads to preterm labor. The monotony of bed rest can also cause added stress, and a woman who is inactive frequently eats less and ultimately could harm her babies even more. Still, the benefits of resting in a reclined position are important for any pregnant woman. A good compromise, therefore, is to rest often—three 30-minute naps per day throughout pregnancy.

Home Monitoring

Another controversial procedure involves home uterine activity monitors (HUAM). Used to detect uterine contractions and the possibility of premature labor, the device is used at home to record subtle contractions and transmits the data over the phone to the physician's office, where it is analyzed. If the information indicates that a woman is in early labor, her doctor may prescribe bed rest or medication to help stop the contractions. HUAM is very expensive and time consuming. In addition, studies examining the benefits of HUAM differ widely. However, some doctors contend, HUAM still helps mothers by educating them in recognizing contractions.

Drug Intervention

These days, doctors have an arsenal of medication to help slow or stop the onset of labor. Some women who experience preterm labor will be hospitalized and treated aggressively with a magnesium sulfate IV and an injection of the steroid Betamethasone to help the babies' lungs mature more quickly and prevent respiratory problems after birth. Once labor has ceased for more than 12 hours, the expectant mother may be allowed to go home but must continue with drug therapy. Drug therapy is also considered controversial by many since it only temporarily halts labor.

TOP FIVE WAYS TO KEEP SANE DURING BED REST

Whether for placenta previa or preterm labor, some women are put on bed rest. It doesn't have to feel like a life sentence, though. Bed rest can be a time to catch up on reading or cuddling older children, who often get lost in the shuffle after twins arrive. Here are some ideas to help make the best of a trying situation.

1. **Rainy-day projects.** Whether it's organizing old photos, mending worn-out socks, or catching up on correspondence, we all have household assignments just waiting for the right time to be completed. Now's your chance. Make a list and then complete one a day.

2. **Movie madness.** Take an informal poll from family and friends of their favorite movies, give the list to your husband, pop some popcorn, then sit back and relax. Now if you could only find the remote!

3. **The write stuff.** Keep a pregnancy journal noting the personality differences of the two baby boxers duking it out in your belly.

4. **Mild exercise.** Contact a physical therapist through your local hospital for a list of simple exercises that you can perform while in bed. Prolonged inactivity is detrimental to your body (as well as your mind).

5. **Education is the key.** Save the romance novels for your next vacation and instead stock up on books educating you on the joys (and headaches) of parenting twins.

• •

IF YOUR BABIES ARE BORN PREMATURELY

I went to see Conner and Ryan every day so I was able to connect with them and develop a bond. I could hold them, though they were attached to wires and all the paraphernalia that goes with the incubators. I made it a point to feed my babies, to bathe them. I went with their schedule. When the nurses said this is bath time, this is such and such, I made it a point to be there to do that for them.

Even with proper prenatal care and an excellent diet, twins sometimes show up a little too early. Seeing your newborns in NICU is frightening, but take some comfort in knowing that there have been great strides in the medical community during the last 30 years that have dramatically raised the survival rate for premature infants. Only a few decades ago, a baby weighing less than 3 pounds had only a 10 percent chance of survival; today it stands at greater than 90 percent. And new records are broken all the time. Still, parents need to prepare both mentally and emotionally in case their twins are born prematurely.

When Babies Need NICU

When twins are born at less than 36 weeks gestation, they are considered premature. Some of their vital organs are not working optimally, so the babies must be taken to a special-care unit in the nursery called the neonatal intensive care unit, or NICU. If the hospital doesn't have such a unit, the babies are quickly transported to a better-equipped medical center. Once there, babies are placed in incubators, are given oxygen and intravenous fluids, and are usually attached to several monitoring devices. The length of their stay will depend on their weight and gestational age, as well as any complications that may arise. Highly trained neonatologists and neonurses tend to their pint-sized patients with great precision and compassion, yet when parents see their babies hooked up to the numerous tubes and high-tech equipment, it can be upsetting. Their babies' appearance doesn't match that of their prenatal fantasy of rosy-cheeked infants. Instead, premature newborns have little body fat and appear helpless and feeble. Disappointment and guilt often set in as parents question their actions of the last months. What went wrong? While understanding that there is nothing that an expectant mother or father could have done to intervene with nature, talking through their feelings with family members, friends, the NICU staff, and members of the clergy can help tremendously and allow parents to come to terms with this highly emotional situation.

Complications Associated with Prematurity

Premature infants are more susceptible to problems arising from low birth weight and prematurity. A variety of respiratory problems can occur, like apnea (when baby stops breathing for more than 15 seconds and must be revived) and respiratory distress syndrome (RDS, when baby's premature lungs lack a chemical called surfactant). In addition, these babies often have a lower resistance to infection. They may develop vision problems or jaundice; or in extreme cases, premature babies may develop neurological defects like cerebral palsy. With relatively little fat on their bodies, premature babies are more prone to dehydration and problems regulating their body temperatures. Tiny infants are often not yet old enough to feed properly, further complicating problems of dehydration and feeding disorders.

TOP FIVE WAYS TO BOND WITH PREMATURE INFANTS

When preemies are confined to incubators, it's often difficult for parents to begin the bonding process with their children. But there are ways for parents to feel close to their infants even while the little ones are temporarily in NICU.

1. **Visit often.** Although recovering from childbirth (cesareans especially) is draining, try to visit your newborns at least once a day. Both you and your babies will benefit greatly.

2. **Nurse your babies.** Yes, it is possible to nurse even premature infants. Speak with the NICU staff concerning feeding schedules. For extremely early arrivals who often have trouble sucking, you may have to express your milk and nurse your twins via feeding tubes. (For more information, read La Leche's Publication No. 26, *Breastfeeding Your Premature Infant*.)

3. **Experience the magic of touch.** Even if you can't hold your babies, your touch and gentle words will begin the parent-child attachment, and research has shown that touching premature babies actually helps them grow healthier.

4. **Understand information is the key.** By asking questions about their care and informing yourself on the needs of premature infants, you will ease your fears. Take an active part in your babies' recovery.

5. **Use a picture to say a thousand words.** Place a photograph of your family inside babies' bassinets along with an article of clothing that you've worn. Your babies will be comforted and begin to associate your scent with you.

• •

Lifestyle Changes

Slow down—women carrying twins hear this often from their obstetricians. It can be a big adjustment for women who are accustomed to living life on the go. But it is important to take things easy for the next nine months. Learn to listen to your body and act according to its needs.

How We Feel

Everything is magnified for women expecting multiples. With the increased hormones that multiple fetuses produce, morning sickness may be heightened. Expect mood swings and moments of irritability. With the extra weight comes pressure on the stomach (causing heartburn), pressure on the lungs (causing breathlessness with every step you take), pressure on the intestinal tract (causing constipation and hemorrhoids), and pressure on the back. Beginning in the middle of the second trimester, expect a degree of pelvic pressure every time you stand. Are you getting the picture? Carrying multiples is a tough job. But just wait, the real work begins once they're born!

Getting Plenty of Rest

As the babies grow and you continue to gain weight, you'll tire more easily and require more rest. Try to arrange for several naps during the day where you can fully recline, preferably on your left side (keeping weight off your lungs and helping organs function better). If you continue to work full time and napping isn't feasible, try to sit in a semi-reclined position with your feet elevated for at least 20 minutes several times a day.

Top Five Comfortable Sleeping Tips for Extremely Pregnant Women

By the third trimester, most women find it impossible to get a good night's sleep—but with a little ingenuity, expectant moms can get some rest. Start by trying these tips.

1. **Try maternity pillows.** These specially made pillows come in all shapes, styles, and sizes and are used to give back support or belly support. Experiment with various positions and styles until you find the right one.

2. **A strategically placed pillow goes a long way.** If you're on a limited budget, try using the pillows you have at home. A pillow wedged in the corner of your back, one between your knees, and one under your stomach give you all the support you'll need. Just don't move in the middle of the night or you'll have to adjust them all over again!

3. **Avoid lying on your back.** While it may be comfortable for some, sleeping on your back can decrease the blood flow to the babies. It will often make you feel lightheaded and therefore is not recommended.

4. **Sleep semi-reclined.** Create a mini-throne of sorts on your bed using lots of pillows. Then sleep semi-reclined with your head resting against the wall or headboard.

5. **Experiment with other types of furniture.** I slept on a soft leather couch during my last month. The cushions molded to my body and the couch back gave me support. Another expectant mom successfully slept for weeks on her living-room recliner.

EXERCISE SENSIBLY

Although exercising helps maintain good circulation and muscle tone, many doctors recommend restricting all aerobic activities around the twentieth week of pregnancy. For some women, vigorous exercise brings on early labor. Yoga, stretching, walking, and swimming are usually acceptable for most women throughout pregnancy unless they experience contractions—when it is advisable to stop.

TOP FIVE EXERCISES FOR EXTREMELY PREGNANT WOMEN

Your doctor has just told you to stop all aerobic exercising. Now what? You still have three months to go before the babies come!

There are plenty of exercises that even a very pregnant woman can do without increasing her chances for preterm labor. Start by trying these stretches. (*Note: Consult your physician first before undertaking any exercise program.*)

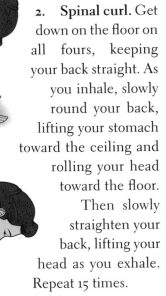

1. **Tailor's sit.** Sit on the floor, legs crossed, arms at side. Straighten your back as you inhale slowly, then exhale and relax your spine. Repeat 10 times. Next, do 10 Kegel exercises by contracting the pelvic floor muscles, tightening as if you were stopping the flow of urine.

2. **Spinal curl.** Get down on the floor on all fours, keeping your back straight. As you inhale, slowly round your back, lifting your stomach toward the ceiling and rolling your head toward the floor. Then slowly straighten your back, lifting your head as you exhale. Repeat 15 times.

3. **Side stretch.** Begin by standing with feet shoulder-width apart, weight centered, arms at your sides. As you inhale, raise your right arm over your shoulder and stretch to your left, lengthening your right leg until your toe is pointed. Hold for 5 seconds. Slowly return to center position as you exhale. Repeat with left arm. Do 15 repetitions.

4. **Wall push-up and calf stretch.** Stand 1 foot from a wall with your hands in front of your shoulders. Bend your elbows and lean forward, touching the wall and making sure to keep your heels firmly on the floor. Slowly push back, letting your arms do all the work. Do 20 repetitions.

5. **Back and hip stretch.** With your left hand lightly touching the top of a chair, bring your right knee to the side of your belly by placing your right hand under your lower thigh. As you raise the knee, bend your left knee slightly and slowly round your back and head. Hold for 5 seconds as you feel your back stretching. Release slowly and repeat 5 times. Switch sides and repeat.

● ●

Is It Okay to Have Sex?

Sexual desire changes as a woman's body changes. As pregnancy progresses, some women have increased sex drives; others feel so fatigued and nauseated that sex is the last thing on their minds. It's not unusual for husbands to feel less amorous toward their wives as well. Often a frank discussion will reveal their fears of hurting the babies. Yet sex during pregnancy can be a great time for togetherness, a way for husbands and wives to connect emotionally. With no need for contraception, lovemaking can be spontaneous. For many, the stress of trying to conceive has been eliminated, enhancing their lovemaking even further. Don't worry about your size, just approach your lovemaking with a sense of humor (not to mention a sense of adventure, since you'll need to be inventive with your lovemaking positions).

To the disappointment of many couples, though, some doctors recommend abstaining from sex during the last trimester since the female orgasm can sometimes increase uterine activity, prompting preterm labor. In addition, semen contains prostaglandin, which can stimulate vaginal contractions. Be sure to discuss your concerns about sexual activity with your doctor.

WHEN TO LEAVE WORK

Doctors' opinions vary regarding the best time for a woman carrying twins to cease working. For some, leaving work around Week 20, as many suggest, will be a welcome treat, while others face a financial hardship if even a day is missed. Planning ahead by working out a pregnancy budget and making saving money a priority will help ease the postpartum financial burden. If your doctor does recommend leaving work before you had initially planned, or if she orders you on bed rest, be sure to check with your benefits counselor at work to see whether you qualify for disability insurance.

STAYING COMFORTABLE

A woman carrying twins in her 30th week is carrying the same weight as a woman carrying a singleton at term. For the mom carrying multiples, during the next 10 weeks (assuming she'll carry her babies to term) comfort becomes harder and harder to achieve. Try the following devices to ease your discomfort.

- **Sandals.** During pregnancy it's not uncommon for feet to increase a full size (and often they don't return to their prepregnancy size after birth). To keep your feet comfortable, wear sandals or a strong pair of flip-flops.

- **Support hose.** It's not just for the senior set anymore. Wearing support hose will help alleviate swelling of the feet and ankles (edema), and aid in the prevention of varicose veins.

- **Belly support.** Toward the end of the second trimester and throughout the third, the weight of the babies on a pregnant woman's back can be intense and painful. Relieve the pressure by wearing a belly support, a mini-girdle that wraps around the lower stomach and back. It is available at most maternity stores and through maternity catalogs (see Appendix).

- **Maternity/nursing bra.** A good maternity bra with flaps that open to enable breastfeeding not only gives support to heavy breasts, decreasing the chances for a backache, but it may also help prevent stretch marks.

- **Maternity pillow.** Essential to a good night's sleep, a maternity pillow should top every pregnant woman's shopping list.

TOP FIVE WAYS TO AVOID UNWANTED ATTENTION

"You must be due any day now!" If I had a nickel for every time I heard that, my kids' college funds would be topping $1 million. Women carrying multiples are *big* and draw lots of attention—sometimes unwanted. If you're averse to public scrutiny over your bulging belly, follow these tips to help keep attention to a minimum.

1. **Wear the proper maternity clothes.** Maternity clothes that cling tightly across an ever-growing stomach might as well have a neon sign flashing, "Look at me!" A better alternative is a high-waisted sun dress with ample material to camouflage your figure. Borrow from other moms or hit the second-hand clothing stores.

2. **Keep it simple.** When a stranger asks, "Are you due soon?" rather than answering with a lengthy explanation justifying your size—just state the obvious, "I'm having twins"—then smile, and walk away.

3. **Carry a prop.** As you walk through a crowded restaurant or department store, a sweater or coat folded across your arms can throw off many an inquisitive stranger.

4. **Avoid eye contact.** With a little practice, you'll be able to spot trouble from the corner of your eye. And if you're quick enough, you can leave the scene before the enemy has a chance to fire the first shot.

5. **Relax and enjoy.** Give up hiding from the public and learn to appreciate the added special attention. After all, it will be gone before you know it.

TRAVELING

Usually, the journey itself isn't harmful to your babies, but with the added chance of preterm labor or other complications that women carrying multiples sometimes experience, most doctors suggest that their patients stay close to home after they reach Week 30.

DIET

The first priority of any mom expecting twins should be sound nutrition. Expectant mothers who have a proper diet end up with babies who weigh more overall. And since the birth weight of twins is an important indicator in predicting their future mental and physical health, it's extremely important for you to eat well. A visit to a nutritionist who specializes in high-risk pregnancies can help mothers-to-be with poor eating habits streamline their diets.

How to Help Avoid Low Birth Weight Through a Proper Diet

Low birth weight (less than 5 pounds, 8 ounces at term) is a serious problem facing moms expecting twins. The good news is that it's also the most preventable problem. While a mother expecting a singleton should consume about 2,600 calories and 100 grams of protein a day, women carrying twins need a *minimum* of 3,100 calories and 130 grams of protein. While it may seem like an incredible goal to reach, the extra calories and protein required are easily met with just one additional quart of milk a day!

Types of Food Needed for a Healthy Pregnancy

The following are merely diet highlights. Consult your physician or nutritionist about her dietary recommendations.

Protein. The amino acids found in protein are essential in building cells and vital in the growth and development of fetal heart, brain, tissue, and muscle.

Lack of adequate protein during pregnancy appears to be strongly connected to low birth weight. In clinical studies conducted as early as the 1940s, Bertha S. Burke, a public health nutritionist at Harvard School of Public Health in Boston, found that when a mother consumed 80 grams or more of protein per day, her baby would weigh at least 6 pounds at birth. Conversely, when a woman received less than

45 grams of protein daily, her baby had a 47 percent chance of weighing less than 5.5 pounds. Burke found that with every additional 10 grams of protein (up to 100 grams per day), the baby's weight would increase by one half pound at birth (*What Every Pregnant Woman Should Know: The Truth About Diet and Drugs in Pregnancy*, 1988).

Meat, fish, dairy, nuts, and legumes offer the best sources of complete protein. Choose sources with a high ratio of protein to fat—in other words, eat broiled fish and skinless chicken instead of fatty or fried red meat. And while it may be tempting to try liquid or powdered protein drinks, avoid them. Strict vegetarians who abstain from meat products should combine protein sources like legumes with whole grains and nuts to obtain complete protein. A protein-rich diet for the vegetarian should also include an abundance of soy products (soy milk, soy yogurt, and tofu).

FOODS HIGH IN PROTEIN

(amounts of protein per serving are averages)

Beef, chicken, liver, pork, turkey . . . . .4 oz.: 21 grams

Salmon, trout, shrimp . . . . .4 oz.: 22 grams

Canned tuna . . . . .4 oz.: 28 grams

Cheddar cheese . . . . .1 oz.: 7 grams

Cottage cheese . . . . .4 oz.: 19 grams

Eggs . . . . .1 egg: 6 grams

Whole milk . . . . .8 oz.: 8 grams

Powdered milk . . . . .1 cup (dry): 25 grams

Yogurt . . . . .1 cup: 8 grams

Peanuts . . . . .4 oz.: 30 grams

Peanut butter . . . . .⅓ cup: 25 grams

Chickpeas (garbanzo beans) . . . . .3½ oz.: 20 grams

Lima beans . . . . .1 cup: 13 grams

Brown rice . . . . .7 oz.: 14 grams

Oats . . . . .3 oz.: 12 grams

Spaghetti . . . . .5 oz.: 12 grams

Broccoli . . . . .1 cup: 5 grams

Spinach (cooked) .1 cup: 5 grams

Corn (cooked) . . . . .1 cup: 5 grams

Iron. During pregnancy your need for iron increases dramatically. Iron is essential in building hemoglobin (red blood cells), which transports oxygen in the blood. Toward the end of pregnancy, a baby's need for iron rises significantly; and if a pregnant mom doesn't maintain a sufficient level, she will develop anemia, a condition that may lead to pregnancy complications. Iron is also important for a baby's nutrition immediately following birth, and therefore it's important to build up a supply prior to his arrival. In addition, it's important to remember that premature babies are often born anemic—another reason to stock up while you can.

Eating iron-rich foods along with foods high in vitamin C will aid in the absorption of the mineral, raising its efficiency in the body. Most women will find it difficult to meet their daily iron requirement through diet alone, so often a physician will suggest taking iron supplements. Take the supplement between meals with a glass of fruit juice or water (avoid taking with milk) to aid in its absorption.

FOODS HIGH IN IRON

(amounts of iron per serving are averages)

Beef . . . . .3 oz.: 2 mg
Chickpeas (garbanzo beans) and . . . . .1 cup: 4 mg
   other legumes (beans and peas)
Clams . . . . .3 oz.: 10 mg
Dried fruit . . . . .10 to 12: 5.5 mg
Raisins . . . . .½ cup: 2.7 mg
Pumpkin seeds . . . . .¼ cup: 3 mg
Soy products (tofu, miso) . . . . .1 cup: 26 mg
Spinach . . . . .1 cup: 4 mg
Wheat germ and other whole grains . . . . .½ cup: 3.3 mg
Other foods high in iron:
Sardines
Sea vegetables (seaweed)
Artichokes

Calcium. If the thought of drinking four glasses of milk a day doesn't turn you on, consider other sources of calcium like cheese, yogurt, almonds, sardines, tuna, salmon, and a variety of green leafy vegetables. Extra calcium is needed in a pregnant woman's diet to aid in the development of fetal bones, teeth, heart, and nerves and to assist in blood clotting. In addition, some studies indicate that extra calcium reduces the risk of preeclampsia. To aid in its absorption, avoid eating calcium-rich foods with caffeine or fibrous foods such as whole-grain products.

Folic Acid. Folic acid, a B vitamin, is not only needed for baby's growth and development and liver efficiency, but well-documented studies indicate that a diet deficient in folic acid may contribute to birth defects (such as cleft palate and spina bifida, a condition where the spinal column doesn't close completely) and low birth weight. Raw green vegetables (parsley, cilantro, chicory, dandelion leaves), whole-grain breads, citrus fruits, and legumes all contain high concentrations of folic acid. Many foods rich in iron and protein also contain folic acid.

Salt and Fats. It used to be that a pregnant woman was put on a low-salt diet, but these days a moderate amount of salt is not only considered safe but encouraged. And while a diet for a woman carrying multiples may appear to be high in fat, it is important in the absorption of vitamins and minerals. Don't shy away from dairy products because of high fat content—instead choose lowfat alternatives.

Vitamin Supplements

Taking a prenatal vitamin everyday doesn't mean you can skip a meal—it simply offers insurance that every essential vitamin and mineral requirement is covered. Some women carrying twins will be advised by their physicians to take several kinds of supplements (iron, calcium, and so on).

Tips on Gaining Enough Weight

Pregnancy is no time to start a diet, but for some women, consuming more than 3,600 calories each day is the equivalent to standing on one foot while skateboarding—in short, a real challenge. Take meal time seriously and consider the following tips to help put on the pounds.

- **Make every meal count.** Forget about fast food, sweets, and junk snacks. Plan your meals carefully, making sure you eat a wide range of healthy, fresh food with an emphasis on protein. Choose foods that are nutritious, given their calorie and fat content. Sour cream may seem like a delicious way to get a serving of dairy, but check the label—it offers little nutritional value. On the other hand, if you feel your diet is too high in fat, substituting lowfat cottage cheese or 1 percent milk is a better alternative than cutting them out completely.

- **Eat many small meals instead of three big ones.** Eating several small meals each day instead of three large ones will keep your energy level high, offer a constant flow of nutrients to growing babies, and eliminate that uncomfortable "stuffed" feeling often associated with eating a large meal.

- **Increase dairy.** Because they are high in protein, calcium, and calories, dairy foods are a quick answer to fulfilling extra caloric and protein requirements.

- **Drink liquids with calories.** Substitute your eight glasses of water each day with broths, fruit juices, or milk.

- **Make a late-night snack tray.** Have a small snack tray of fruit slices, cheese, or peanut butter and crackers by your bed so that when you get up in the middle of the night to use the bathroom (which is usually several times a night), you can grab a quick bite.

- **Bag it.** Whether it's a short trip to the supermarket or an afternoon drive in the country, be sure to keep a supply of nutritious snacks in the car.

- **Accessorize your food.** Grated cheese or chopped roasted peanuts sprinkled on a salad add not only flavor but a nice little protein kick.

- **Disguise foods you dislike.** Can't stand eggs or milk? Hide them in delicious dishes like creamed soups, cream sauces, French toast, or even chocolate milk.

Importance of Fluids

Not only is getting enough food important for a woman expecting twins, so is drinking enough fluids. Drinking at least eight glasses of liquid a day eases constipation and reduces the risk of a urinary tract infection. Your body needs the extra fluid to help transport nutrients to your babies, build cells, and remove waste from both your system and the babies'. The added fluid builds additional blood, amniotic fluid, and tissue.

Taboos

The dangers of smoking have been known for years, but the hazards of tobacco are magnified even more during pregnancy. Not only does smoking while pregnant put your life at risk by increasing your chances for heart disease and cancer, but it also has been associated with low birth weight, placenta previa, miscarriages, sudden infant death syndrome (SIDS), and even preterm labor.

Another taboo to avoid during pregnancy is alcohol. Women who drink during pregnancy often have children with fetal alcohol syndrome, a serious condition that includes mental retardation, growth deficiencies, and abnormalities. Various conflicting reports on how much alcohol during pregnancy is safe are inconclusive—so once again, a pregnant mom should err on the side of caution and omit alcohol completely from her lifestyle.

Cutting down on or cutting out coffee and other caffeinated beverages during pregnancy is also a good idea. While not nearly as dangerous as alcohol or smoking, recent studies suggest that a stimulant drug such as caffeine may not be safe during pregnancy.

And of course, the use of illegal drugs such as marijuana and cocaine are potential time bombs to a pregnant woman. Avoid them at all costs.

TOP FIVE DELICIOUS RECIPES TO
HELP BEEF UP YOUR BABIES

When planning your diet, remember that protein, protein, protein adds weight to your babies. Try for a minimum of 130 grams of pro-

tein each day to ensure that your babies have the best chance of
being born big and plump!

....

KUNG PAO CHICKEN WITH BROCCOLI

Serves 4
38 grams of protein per serving

*When I was pregnant, I couldn't get enough of this simple-to-prepare
stir-fry dish. Thinly sliced beef or fresh shrimp works well with it, too.*

> 1 tbsp. soy sauce
> 1 tsp. cooking wine
> 1 tsp. rice vinegar
> 1 tbsp. water
> 2 tsp. cornstarch
> 3 tbsp. peanut oil
> 4 skinless, boneless chicken breasts (about 1 lb. total),
>   cut into 1-inch cubes
> 2 cups broccoli, flowers and tender stalks, cut up
> 2 dried chili peppers
> 5 green onions, chopped
> 1 cup dry-roasted peanuts, chopped
> Fresh cilantro, chopped, for garnish

1. Prepare stir-fry sauce by combining soy sauce, cooking wine,
   rice vinegar, water, and cornstarch in a small bowl. Mix well
   and set aside.

2. Heat 1 tbsp. of peanut oil in wok or large, heavy fry pan. Add
   chicken and sauté until thoroughly cooked, about 5 minutes.
   Remove from pan and set aside.

3. Heat 1 tbsp. of peanut oil in same wok or pan and sauté
   broccoli until tender but crisp, about 2 minutes. Remove from
   pan and set aside.

4. Heat remaining 1 tbsp. of peanut oil in same wok or pan and sauté chili peppers until fragrant, about 10 seconds. Add chopped green onions, sauté quickly, then add chopped peanuts. Mix until flavors are well blended, about 30 seconds.

5. Add chicken and broccoli to the chili pepper mixture, then add stir-fry sauce. Quickly toss until sauce thickens and meat and vegetables are well coated. Remove from heat.

6. Serve over steamed rice and garnish with fresh chopped cilantro.

....

YOGURT SHAKE

Serves 2
14 grams of protein per serving

This creamy fruit drink is a great accompaniment to breakfast, or a satisfying midmorning snack. If frozen mangoes are not available, any frozen fruit will do nicely.

> ½ cup chopped frozen mango
> ½ cup frozen berries (raspberries or strawberries)
> 1 banana, peeled and chopped
> ½ cup orange juice
> ½ cup powdered milk
> 2 cups plain yogurt

1. Place fruit and orange juice in blender or food processor. Blend well until fruit is liquefied, about 1 minute.

2. Add powdered milk. Mix well.

3. Add yogurt and blend until smooth, about 30 seconds.

4. Serve in tall, frosted glasses.

....

MOM'S EGG SALAD SANDWICH

Serves 2

20 grams of protein per serving

My mother-in-law told me that when she was pregnant with her first son, Mark, she craved egg salad sandwiches and ate at least one a day. Here she shares her tasty recipe. With such a protein boost, it's no wonder that Mark tipped the scales at more than 10 pounds!

> 3 hard-boiled eggs, shelled and chopped
> ⅓ cup mayonnaise
> 2 tbsp. red onion, finely chopped
> ¼ cup celery, chopped
> 1 tsp. dill
> 1 tsp. Dijon-style mustard
> Salt and pepper to taste

Mix all ingredients until well blended and serve on whole wheat toast.

....

CHARLIE'S SANDWICH

Serves 1

28 grams of protein per serving

My husband's best friend and exercise buddy has been concocting strange sandwiches for as long as we've known him. He chose to share this one for its particularly high protein content. It's also his favorite.

> 2 slices multigrain bread, toasted
> 2 tbsp. creamy peanut butter
> 2 slices Swiss cheese
> Mustard to taste
> 2 thin slices tomato
> 1 leaf romaine lettuce

1. On one side of toasted bread, spread peanut butter.

2. Place cheese directly on top of peanut butter, then dress with a thin layer of mustard.

3. Add sliced tomato and lettuce.

4. To help hold the sandwich together, spread either peanut butter or mustard on remaining slice of bread. Serve immediately.

....

NACHOS

Serves 1
29 grams of protein per serving

Another one of my afternoon pregnancy obsessions, nachos are rich in protein and satisfying to the palate—but watch out for the high fat content of sour cream.

> ⅓ cup refried beans
> 2 oz. tortilla chips (about 30 chips)
> 3 oz. cheddar cheese, grated
> ¼ cup tomato, chopped
> ¼ cup avocado, chopped
> 2 tbsp. red onion, chopped
> 6 black olives, chopped
> Chopped fresh cilantro
> Salsa
> Sour cream (optional)

1. Preheat oven to 375°F. In a small microwave-safe bowl, heat beans in microwave until warm. Stir until creamy.

2. Lay out the tortilla chips on a baking sheet. Carefully spread warm beans on top. Sprinkle cheese on top of beans. Bake in oven until cheese is melted, about 4 to 5 minutes.

3. Remove from oven and slide onto serving plate. Top with tomato, avocado, onion, olives, and cilantro. Dress with salsa and sour cream, if desired. Serve immediately.

Tips for Increasing Chances of a Healthy Pregnancy

- **Diet.** Follow a healthy diet high in calcium, iron, folic acid, and especially protein. Vary your food consumption to be sure that you're getting a variety of nutrients, and eat plenty of fresh fruits and vegetables.

- **Rest.** Don't wait until your doctor puts you on mandatory bed rest— rest often by either napping frequently or putting your feet up for 30 minutes at least three times a day.

- **Prenatal care.** Never miss a doctor's appointment. Read everything you can on multiple pregnancies. Ask questions and discuss your concerns with your physician.

- **Fluids.** Drink, drink, drink, and then drink more (water, juice, and milk).

- **Precautions.** Don't wait until you're exhausted to rest, or starving to eat. Use your common sense when it comes to caring for your body. Avoid alcohol, don't smoke or take any kind of drugs, and always wear your seatbelt while driving. To avoid unnecessary radiation, sit at least 10 feet from the television and stay away from microwave ovens that are in use.

- **Listen to your body.** No one knows the patient better than you. Learn to listen to your body and promptly respond to its needs.

One Final Thought

Being pregnant with twins takes a lot of work and diligence on your part to ensure a healthy outcome, but it's just nature's way of mentally preparing you for what lies ahead. After the birth of your twins, you'll soon realize that pregnancy was the easy part.

•3•

It's All in the Planning

"Why do it today when you can put it off until tomorrow?" While this sentiment is typically the battle cry for busy parents, expectant parents of twins should take the opposite approach—do it *now* or you may never get it done! Around the seventh month of pregnancy, start thinking about setting up your nursery. Shop early for clothes and furniture just in case your little bundles of joy arrive sooner than expected. If your home needs some alterations to accommodate two extra people (as ours did), don't wait until babies are tucked snugly in their cribs before you start getting contract bids. Plan ahead and you'll be all the happier for it.

Nursery Essentials

People would often say to me, "Oh, my baby never used the swing," or "Oh, it was heaven. I loved it." So you never know what your babies will want, need, or enjoy.

Two of everything? Many parents of twins say, "not necessarily." Before you break the bank with needless infant equipment, it makes better economic sense to buy only one of all the baby extras like swings and snugly sacks, then wait and see how your babies respond to each. This way you won't be stuck with more than you need. If, for instance, you find by the second week that you can't survive without two swings, run out and buy another.

CRIB

Probably the most impor-
tant piece of equip-
ment, the crib is the
focal point of every
nursery. No need to
buy or borrow two
right away—twins can
easily sleep together for the
first six months (and sometimes
longer). When your babies begin to
roll and move (around 4 months of
age), however, you will need to take steps
to deter them from disturbing each other's sleep. A rolled-up blanket
or padded bumper (available through catalogs and some baby stores)
anchored down the center of the crib keeps everyone on his own side.
With the recent rise in twinning, some companies are even manufac-
turing compact double cribs (see Appendix).

BOUNCER SEATS

For those moments between feeding, sleeping, and cuddling, bouncer
seats are a great place for babies to check out their new world while
parents catch their breath. Some seats have vibrating motors that
gently soothe babies to sleep (my kids spent many a night in theirs).
One mail order company actually makes a double bouncer seat (see
Appendix).

CAR SEATS

By law, each twin needs his own car seat while riding in an automobile. Infants up to 20 pounds need a rear-facing seat, while toddlers
weighing 20 to 40 pounds require a front-facing car seat. Styles and
prices range dramatically, but to save money, consider buying a car seat
that converts from rear-facing to front-facing. If you purchase this
dual model, you'll only need to buy two seats instead of four. There
is a drawback, however. If you buy front-facing seats, you'll also need

to buy infant carriers to help you transport your babies in and out of the house. (Big and bulky, front-facing seats aren't portable.) Rear-facing car seats are small, are easy to remove from the car, and can act as infant carriers, enabling one parent to transport both babies from the house to the car in one trip—an important consideration when the parent is alone and doesn't want to leave a baby unattended. In addition, rear-facing models allow parents to take snoozing infants directly from the car into restaurants and such without removing them from their seats and disturbing their slumber.

STROLLER

Just a few years ago, parents expecting twins had a difficult time locating a double stroller. These days, however, choices abound. The limousine style, or tandem stroller, where one baby sits in front of the other, makes maneuvering through doorways easy. One drawback— only the baby in back can fully recline for a nap on the go; the baby in front is left to nap in an upright position. Side-by-side strollers, on the other hand, are lighter and more compact than the tandem style, but many don't offer enough back support for tiny infants, and tight store aisles as well as doorways pose a maneuverability problem. The third type of double stroller, where babies face each other, is difficult to find in most retail stores—and as your kids grow, the face-to-face position can encourage sibling squabbles.

SWING

A lifesaver for many parents, a swing gently calms even the fussiest baby. But should you purchase two? Considering the expense (swings run anywhere from $80 to $100) and space, many parents say no. Instead, buy one now and take a wait-and-see approach.

CLOTHING

Although most friends and family will give you clothes in duplicate, your twins' wardrobe need not be twice that of a single baby. Each needs her own jacket, shoes, and hat, but they can share play clothes and pajamas.

TOP FIVE WARDROBE ESSENTIALS
AND EXPENDABLES

• •

Once the baby shower is over, take inventory of your twins' wardrobe and fill in those gaping fashion holes before your babies arrive. But shop carefully—baby clothes are expensive.

1. **Essential: one-piece stretch suits.** During the first few weeks, make life easy on yourself and dress babies in comfortable cotton stretch suits. They'll keep your little ones warm, they launder great, and have no clumsy buttons or zippers.

2. **Expendable: matching outfits.** Okay, maybe just one set for that special first photograph, but for everyday wear, matching outfits are a waste of money.

3. **Essential: cotton onesies.** Perfect if you live in a warm climate or your babies are born in the summer, these one-piece T-shirts are cool, crisp, and comfortable.

4. **Expendable: booties and mittens.** If you take your twins out in cool weather, forget booties and mittens and instead dress them in one-piece stretch suits, then wrap them snugly in wool blankets.

5. **Essential: hats.** Protect delicate bald heads and necks from the sun with brimmed hats.

• •

BLANKETS

Infants require plenty of blankets—light cotton for swaddling (3 to 4 each), wool afghan for strolling (2 each), soft flannel to place on the floor for playtime (1 each), and colorful receiving blankets (1 each). While 14 blankets may seem too many, it will save you from having to do laundry every day.

Toys

For the first six months, most babies don't have much interest in toys, but around 3 months of age they will enjoy batting at a play gym. You'll need only one—babies are small enough to be placed side by side underneath.

Diapers

Count on using 150 a week for the first few months. But should you use cloth or disposable? Each has its benefits and pitfalls. Here's what parents have to say.

Benefits of Cloth Diapers

- Environmentally, cloth is the winner. Before they are toilet trained, your twins will use between 16,000 to 20,000 diapers. That's a lot of trash!

  The huge environmental impact of disposables didn't really hit me until I had to empty a trash can filled with one day's worth of used disposables. I felt so guilty. I called a diaper service the next day.

- Most services deliver fresh cloth diapers every week directly to your door so you'll never run out.

- Cloth diapers breathe, preventing diaper rash.

Disadvantages of Cloth Diapers

- You must purchase plastic covers at a cost of $5 each (you'll need about five for each baby). And as your babies grow, you'll need to purchase larger sizes.

- They are not as absorbent as disposables and often shift inside their covers, leading to messy leaks and countless daily cleanups.

Benefits of Disposables

- Easy to use—no diaper folding or Velcro covers involved.

  Before we had Alyssa and Katelyn, we decided on cloth. After we had the babies, we quickly switched to disposables. It got to

the point where I needed to do what I needed to do to survive.
And disposables were a lot easier.

- Great for traveling. Unlike cloth, disposables are easy to discard while on the road. (Just be sure to use a trash can.)

Disadvantages of Disposables

- Disposables create an excessive amount of garbage both in your home and in our nation's burgeoning landfills.

- The plastic outer lining doesn't breathe. Couple that with excess moisture buildup due to disposables' absorbability and the result for most babies is a nasty diaper rash.

Most parents say the cost comparison balances out. While the unit cost per cloth diaper is cheaper than disposables, cloth requires more frequent changing. In addition, parents need to buy at least 10 covers ($50) every few months. Looking for a compromise? Use cloth during the day while at home and then switch to disposables for outings and nighttime.

Baby Monitor

Not just for nighttime, baby monitors permit mobility—a must for house-bound parents. While the twins nap, take the monitor outside and do a little gardening or relax in the sunshine. It'll feel like a mini-vacation.

Washer and Dryer

Before my twins arrived, I did about two loads of wash a week. Now I do close to five! I couldn't imagine trudging off daily to the laundromat with my boys to do laundry. These days manufacturers make all sorts of models—big and small—to fit any budget. It might be a financial stretch for some, but remember that free time is precious and there's a lot to be said for buying a piece of sanity.

Music Box

It may seem minor, but when you have two screaming babies and only two hands, a soothing melody can work miracles on fussy babies.

SNUGLY SACK

Single or double, a snugly sack is worn across your chest, keeping baby close and happy and your hands free.

PLAYPEN/PORT-A-CRIB

A playpen (also known as a port-a-crib) is a safe haven to place a calm baby while you soothe his not-so-calm sister. Or use it as a play area while doing *another* load of laundry. Don't expect to use it as a playpen past the first year, though. Once they become mobile, most babies protest when placed inside. But it's still a useful investment if you're a family on the go. A playpen is lightweight and compact, and therefore useful as a crib for overnight traveling (if you need two, borrow the second from a family member or friend).

FUTURE NURSERY ITEMS

No need to buy everything before the babies arrive. Many nursery items aren't necessary until twins reach 6 months or older.

High Chairs or Tot Locks

Once the twins start on solid foods (between 4 and 6 months), it's time to think about high chairs. Some parents opt for one and feed their babies in shifts. We chose to buy two tot locks (small, folding chairs that clamp directly onto a table) instead. They're less expensive (around $35 for a tot lock versus $100 for a high chair), they save space (a big consideration for my cramped residence), and they're portable. Since we take them everywhere, we never have to worry about finding two high chairs when we go to a restaurant or visit family.

Umbrella Strollers/Travel Strollers

When twins begin to walk, many rebel against sitting in their double stroller—it's too confining. Two single umbrella or travel strollers offer a solution by allowing babies to sit upright in full view of everything. Umbrella strollers are also more compact than double strollers, making them perfect for traveling. Some parents find that buying two single strollers allows for various combinations: one parent, one twin;

two parents, two twins; one parent, two twins (one in stroller, one in backpack; or, clamp them together with a specially made clip—see Appendix—to make a double stroller).

Top Five Twin Gadgets

Just like professional chefs, families with twins know that the secret to success is in the tools they use. Here's a nursery list of five favorites to help life run smoothly.

1. **Nurse Mate double nursing pillow** (Four Dee Products, $39.95). New moms say that breastfeeding two babies at once is not only easy, but saves lots of time. The pillow wraps around your waist like a giant donut, allowing plenty of room for both babies to rest comfortably on top.

2. **Backpack diaper bag** (Eagle Creek Travel Gear, $35). When both hands are occupied with precious cargo, there's no room to share a shoulder with a diaper bag. Eagle Creek's backpack diaper bag has a built-in changing table and plastic-lined pockets. Moms also like the fact that it doesn't look like a typical bunny-decorated diaper bag.

3. **Gemini baby carrier** (Tot Tenders Baby Products, $55). When a stroller or car seat is too bulky, or babies simply want to be held close, Gemini's double sack allows moms or dads to carry both babies at once; or use separately—one baby for each parent.

4. **Graco "tandem-style" stroller** (Graco, $99). Moms say a tandem-style stroller (one baby in front of the other) makes maneuvering through doorways much easier than a side-by-side baby stroller.

5. **Medela electric double breast pump** (Medela, $30 per month). Have two bottles of breast milk ready for the baby-sitter

in less than 10 minutes. The time you save pumping both breasts at once more than pays for the $1-a-day rental fee (less expensive for long-term rentals).

• •

Two for the Price of One? Money Matters

For families who are suddenly surprised to find that two babies are on the way instead of just one, saving money becomes a major priority. And while it will ultimately cost more to raise twins (start those college savings accounts now!), the good news is that there are ways for parents of multiples to make their pennies go further.

When we first learned that we were having twins, my pragmatic husband quipped, "Will we get a deal on our hospital bill?" Actually, the answer is yes and no. Physicians do charge more for a twin delivery than a singleton delivery, but the cost for prenatal visits and delivery is not double the price. The amount of your hospital room will remain the same as that for a singleton delivery, but your nursery bill and pediatrician visit will cost double.

When looking into day care centers and mommy-and-me classes, it's a nice surprise to learn that many offer 50 percent discounts when enrolling a second child at the same time. So you see, it does pay to have twins!

REEVALUATE YOUR BUDGET

Before you give up your weekly night out with your spouse in an effort to save some cash, consider reevaluating some fixed expenses in your family budget. First, think about refinancing your mortgage. Even if you can shave off only 1 percent, it could be worth hundreds of dollars annually if you're planning on staying in your present home for more than a few years. And did you know that nearly one third of American homes are assessed higher than their worth? If you feel that your house is overvalued, call your county tax assessor for a reassessment. You could also save nearly 10 percent a year on homeowners and auto insurance by simply raising your deductible to $500 or $1,000.

Health care is another area worth investigating. Check out HMO (health maintenance organization) plans where you can rack up savings of up to 20 percent over traditional PPO (preferred provider organization) plans. Most HMOs include well-baby coverage where the member makes a small copayment with each visit, compared to a PPO plan where the member pays 20 percent of the cost once a deductible has been met. And since the average child visits his pediatrician more than six times during the first year of life (double that with twins), an HMO policy could save a hefty sum of money. Before making any decision, though, speak with your benefits counselor at your company to decide which is best for your family. If you are self-employed or unemployed, call your insurance agent or health care company for more information and a cost comparison of plans.

DOUBLE-DUTY ITEMS

With a little imagination, you'd be surprised at what you can use in multiple ways. Forget about a portable plastic tub or tub ring—try bathing babies in the kitchen sink. When they outgrow the sink, place small, square laundry baskets in the bathtub and put babies inside. The water flows freely through the baskets while keeping babies in an upright position. When the twins are old enough to sit in the tub on their own, use the baskets for toy chests or what they were created for—laundry.

Thinking of buying a changing table? How about spreading a large towel on the floor or on top of a bed instead? We saved money by buying a thick changing pad and placing it on top of our dresser. If you need to furnish your home, think about buying baby furniture with a future. What will you do with the $200 changing table in two years? Probably store it in the attic for the next 20. An antique dry sink (look in the newspaper, scour flea markets or second-hand furniture stores) padded with colorful baby bumpers works just as well, and in a few years you'll have a lovely piece of furniture to use in another part of your home. Instead of a brightly painted nursery rocker, we bought a more mainstream mission-style rocking chair that now sits proudly in our living room.

BREASTFEEDING

Not only is breastfeeding better for your babies, it also saves lots of money. The average newborn drinks up $60 worth of formula each month. Multiply that by two and you have enough for a car payment (and a car might come in handy now).

DO IT YOURSELF

Good with a needle and thread? Why not sew your own baby bumpers and crib blankets? When it's time to introduce solid foods to your twins, make your own baby food. While it's much easier just to open a jar (and on many a tired evening I did), you'll save plenty by making your own. Check out your local bookstore or library for parenting books that contain simple recipes.

Save more money by making your own baby wipes. Start with a roll of top-quality paper towels, baby oil, water, and a round plastic container with a lid. With a sharp knife, slice the towel roll into two equal halves. Place one half in the plastic container and store the second half for future use. Slowly drizzle ⅓ cup baby oil evenly on top of the towels and then add 2 cups of water. Seal the container for approximately one hour to aid in the absorption. If the towels are too dry, add a few tablespoons of water; if too moist, simply leave the lid off for an hour or two.

FREEBIES AND COUPONS

Many corporations like Gerber, Beechnut, and Kimberly Clark offer coupons and free samples of baby food, diapers, and formula to families with multiples (for complete list, see Appendix). Call your local Midas dealer for discounted Century 1000 car seats. Return the car seats after use and Midas will give you a brake service coupon good for the price of the car seats.

Want to get out of the house with your spouse but are concerned about spending money? Many organizations (including Mothers of Twins Club) raise money by selling coupon books, chock-full of discounts on movie tickets and two-for-one deals at local eateries.

SECOND-HAND ROSE

When it was time to get a second crib (our boys shared one crib for the first six months), we hit the used furniture stores. We saved more than 50 percent on a previously owned crib. With a little scrubbing, our used crib looked as good as new. One shrewd mom I know scanned the newspapers in search of baby furniture and found a crib, changing table, glider, and ottoman for less than $300. Another money-saving tip is to join your local Mothers of Twins Club and make a killing at their semiannual clothing exchanges.

ONE MORE THING . . .

Don't get stuck on name brands, which are often expensive, when store brands will do the same trick. Know how much things cost, and remember that a sale isn't always a bargain. With a little common sense and some careful planning, having twins doesn't have to send you to the poorhouse.

Getting the Family Ready for Twins

The crib is in place, the curtains are hung—now what?

THE BIRTH EXPERIENCE

When Verna went into labor, we had no idea that there were twins. There was no ultrasound in those days. After Verna gave birth, the doctor came out to the waiting room. He was all excited. "Hey, Bill," he said. "What do you want? A boy or a girl?" And I said, "Gee, I don't know. I just want a healthy baby." Then he said, "You've got to make a choice. Do you want a boy or a girl?" So I thought for a moment and I said, "I'll take a boy." Then the doctor made a signal to the nurse and she came out carrying Bruce. I was so happy, but then the doctor said, "You had a hard time deciding what you wanted. You know, it would really be a lot simpler if you had a girl, too. What if we could fix you up with another one?" Then he gave a signal to another nurse and she came out carrying Gale. I was flabbergasted. The doctor was just as excited as I was because he didn't know that Verna was going to have twins. He said, "You know, I can never pick up that second heartbeat." We were all very excited. It was big news.

Enroll in Childbirth Classes

Whether you choose Lamaze, Bradley, or Grantly Dick-Read, childbirth classes help expectant moms (and dads) ease the fear and pain of childbirth through knowledge and relaxation techniques. Instructors also speak on prenatal education and participants are encouraged to voice concerns and ask questions. While most parents expecting a singleton take the class during the eighth month of pregnancy, book yours earlier just in case the kids make an unscheduled arrival.

Take CPR

Taking an infant CPR (cardiopulmonary resuscitation) class not only prepares you for an emergency, but gives you the confidence you'll need if your babies are born prematurely. Contact your local hospital or Red Cross for a list of class locations.

Tour the Hospital

Call the hospital where you'll be giving birth to set up a tour. Usually offered in the evenings, the tour will give you a sense of familiarity and help to ease your anxieties when the big day arrives. You'll have plenty of opportunity to ask questions. And remember to ask to see the NICU.

Make a Birth Plan

Although your birth plan will probably change many times during the course of labor (pain has a way of transforming even the meekest woman into a bossy tyrant), it's important to have a vision of how you want your labor and subsequent delivery to go. Do you want pain medication? What family members would you like present during delivery? How do you feel about perineal preparation (shaving of the pubic hair)? It's a good idea to make three separate plans: one for a vaginal delivery, one for a cesarean delivery, and one for a premature delivery, since all three are possible.

TOP FIVE METHODS OF PRENATAL BONDING

No need to wait until their birth to get to know your babies—bonding can begin prenatally as soon as you feel the first kick.

1. **Smile for the camera.** Keep all ultrasound photos handy (do like other proud parents and display them on the refrigerator) and look at them often. Try to visualize what your twins will look like.

2. **Who's who?** Differentiate between the two babies wrestling in your belly by trying to distinguish between heads and toes. If you tune in to your body you may find that Baby A is a night owl, while Baby B is an early riser, or that Baby A always gets the hiccups while Baby B prefers to kick you in the groin. (You'd be surprised at how little their personalities change after their birth.)

3. **Refer to them by name.** If none have been chosen, make up pet names.

4. **The magic of touch.** Touch or stroke your belly often and talk to your babies about your hopes and dreams for their future. And remind them to eat!

5. **Write on.** Keep a pregnancy journal in which to note your feelings, the progress of your prenatal check-ups, and each baby's movements.

. . . .

TOP FIVE ESSENTIAL ITEMS TO TAKE TO THE HOSPITAL
. . . .

Your favorite nightgown, your Frank Sinatra CD, and baby clothes. What else do you need? Plenty. Be prepared with this list of must-have gear.

1. **Food for Dad.** Don't overlook the coach. Since hospital cafeterias close early, and labor could happen at 2 A.M., pack a small cooler with sandwiches, fruit, and beverages.

2. **Insurance cards, checkbook, and emergency cash.** You might be concentrating on the birth, but some hospital administrators are concerned with paperwork. Don't be caught off-guard.

3. **The good news list.** After the excitement and exhaustion of giving birth, you won't remember who you have to call. Make a list of names and phone numbers in descending order from most important—Grandma and Grandpa—to the "maybe laters," like Great-Aunt Lucy in Topeka.

4. **Extra batteries.** Whether it's for a flash camera or a portable tape player, have plenty of batteries packed (hospitals don't allow you to plug any electronic equipment into their outlets).

5. **Play things.** Believe it or not, sometimes there's a little downtime during labor. It's best to keep yourself (and your partner) occupied by playing cards, reading a book, or playing a game.

. . . .

Select a Pediatrician

The relationship between you and your pediatrician is an important one. Your twins will visit her at least six times during the first year of life (more if they get sick). To find a reliable candidate, ask friends or contact your local Mothers of Twins Club for recommendations. Many local hospitals offer a doctor referral line as well. Since twins have a higher chance of visiting the doctor more often than singletons simply because there are two of them, be sure to choose a pediatrician who is close to home. After you've selected two or three prospects, set up a get-acquainted appointment where you can meet the doctor and ask questions. Some physicians charge for this service, but many insurance companies will pick up the tab.

Cook Ahead

Stock your freezer with plenty of nutritious reheatable meals. During those first chaotic weeks after the babies are born, cooking will be the last thing on your mind. (Okay, making love will be the last thing on your mind, but cooking runs a close second-to-last.)

Top Five Easy Make-Ahead Meals

· ·

Cooking plenty of one-dish dinners, sealing them in plastic bags, and stocking them away in the freezer will be the best pregnancy gift that you'll give to yourself. Your only regret will be that you didn't make more. Here's a list of my favorites.

· ·

My Meatballs and Tomato Sauce

Serves 6 to 8

Trust me on this one; I'm an Italian American who grew up in my grandfather's restaurant. Serve this with your favorite pasta (spaghetti would be my choice) and if you have the energy, make a green salad.

SAUCE

¼ cup olive oil
2 cloves garlic, crushed
½ carrot, peeled and diced
2 28-oz. cans plum tomatoes, partially drained
¼ cup red wine
2 bay leaves
2 tsp. dried Greek oregano
Salt and pepper to taste

MEATBALLS

2 lbs. ground beef (minimum 15 percent fat; bad for
   the heart, great for taste)
½ cup seasoned bread crumbs
¼ cup onion, finely chopped
2 eggs
⅓ cup Romano or Parmesan cheese, finely grated
¼ cup fresh parsley, chopped
Pinch of dried Greek oregano
Salt and pepper to taste

1. For the sauce, heat oil in heavy stockpot. Add garlic and
   carrots and sauté for several minutes, being careful not to
   burn the garlic.

2. Drain off excess juice from plum tomatoes and add to garlic
   mixture. Pour in wine.

3. Add spices. Simmer for 1 hour.

4. Meanwhile, preheat oven to 350°F, and in a large mixing
   bowl add all meatball ingredients.

5. With clean hands, mix ingredients until well blended.

6. Form golf-ball-sized meatballs with your hands, being careful
   not to pack too tightly. Place on lightly greased pan.

7. Bake in oven, turning only once, for 7 to 10 minutes
   (meatballs will finishing cooking in sauce).

8. When sauce is done, pour through sieve or food grinder into another large pot. Discard seeds and stems, but make sure you have pushed tomato pulp through sieve (otherwise, the sauce will be too thin).

9. Add meatballs to pureed sauce. Adjust seasonings and cook for an additional 20 minutes.

10. Place pot in the refrigerator to cool, then transfer meatballs and sauce to freezer bags and place in the freezer.

11. To serve, defrost in refrigerator. Simmer contents on stove over low heat for 15 minutes, or until meatballs are heated through. Serve with pasta.

....

CHICKEN POT PIE

Makes 2 6-inch pies

This classic one-dish meal is a new parent's dream—just defrost and bake.

PIE CRUST

3 cups flour
Dash of salt
¾ cup chilled unsalted butter
5–6 tbsp. chilled water

PIE FILLING

6 skinless chicken thighs
1 large onion, chopped into 1-inch chunks
2 potatoes, peeled and cut into 1-inch cubes
2 carrots, peeled and cut into ½-inch slices
¼ cup frozen peas
4 tbsp. butter
¼ lb. button mushrooms, quartered

2 tbsp. flour
¾ cup cream
1 tsp. dried savory
Salt and pepper to taste

1. Sift flour and salt into large mixing bowl. Add chilled butter, and, with pastry blender or two knives, cut butter into flour until mixture resembles cornmeal.

2. Mix in water, one tablespoon at a time, until dough holds together.

3. Wrap dough in plastic and chill in refrigerator for 1 hour.

4. Meanwhile, place chicken thighs in medium-size stockpot and fill with water until thighs are covered. Bring to boil over high heat and skim off foam. Reduce heat and simmer for 20 to 30 minutes.

5. Remove chicken from pot. Tear off meat and cut into bite-size pieces, then place in large bowl. Return bones to stockpot.

6. Over medium heat, cook onion, potatoes, carrots, and peas in batches (so all vegetables are fully immersed in stock) until vegetables are tender, about 10 minutes. Add to cooked chicken.

7. In small frying pan, heat 1 tbsp. butter and add mushrooms. Cook until golden, about 5 minutes. Add to chicken mixture.

8. In same pan, add remaining butter and flour and stir constantly until well blended, about 1 minute. Pour in about ½ cup of chicken stock and stir until thickened. Remove from heat and stir in cream. Stir into chicken mixture.

9. Add the savory, as well as salt and pepper to taste.

10. To prepare crusts, remove dough from plastic and divide into four uneven pieces, making sure bottoms are slightly larger than tops.

11. On well-floured board, roll out bottoms to fit 2 6-inch pie pans. Fill with chicken mixture and cover with tops. Crimp edges and cut several vent holes.

12. Wrap well with aluminum foil and freeze immediately.

13. To cook, thaw pie in refrigerator. Preheat oven to 450°F. Cook pie uncovered for 15 minutes. Lower heat to 350°F and cook for an additional 30 minutes, or until heated inside.

....

TURKEY CHILI

Serves 4

Always a crowd pleaser, this chili recipe calls for ground turkey, a healthier alternative to beef.

> 2 tbsp. olive oil
> 2 cloves garlic, minced
> 1 large onion, chopped
> 1½ lb. ground turkey
> ¼ cup cream
> 2 tbsp. chili powder
> 1 tbsp. dried oregano
> 1 tbsp. lemon juice
> 2 tsp. dried dill
> 1 tbsp. Dijon mustard
> 2 28-oz. cans plum tomatoes, drained
> 1 15-oz. can red kidney beans, drained
> ¼ cup fresh parsley, finely chopped
> 1 cup black olives, sliced

1. In large stockpot, heat oil over medium heat and add garlic and onion, cooking until they are translucent and fragrant, about 3 minutes. Add turkey, crumbling into pieces. Sauté, stirring occasionally until turkey is cooked completely, about 10 minutes.

2. Lower heat and add cream. Simmer until cream is absorbed, about 5 minutes.

3. Add chili powder, oregano, lemon juice, dill, and mustard. Stir until well blended.

4. Add drained tomatoes and simmer for 30 minutes, stirring occasionally. Then add drained kidney beans and cook for an additional 10 minutes.

5. To finish, add chopped parsley and olives. Mix well.

6. Remove pot from heat and place in refrigerator. When cooled, pour into freezer bag and place in freezer.

7. To serve, thaw chili in refrigerator. Simmer over low heat for 15 minutes and serve over steamed rice.

....

PESTO SAUCE

Serves 4 to 6

Another Italian specialty that's easy to make and freezes superbly. The trick is to not add the cheese until you are ready to use the sauce.

> 2 cups fresh basil leaves
> 1 large clove garlic
> ½ to ¾ cup olive oil
> 1 tbsp. pine nuts
> Salt and pepper to taste
> ⅓ cup Parmesan or Romano cheese, finely grated

1. In large food processor or blender, pulse basil and garlic until the basil turns to a paste and the garlic is finely chopped.

2. With machine on, slowly drizzle in olive oil. Blend until pesto becomes a smooth paste.

3. Add pine nuts and pulse until nuts are finely chopped. Add salt and pepper to taste, but do not add cheese!

4. Pour mixture into small freezer bag and place in the freezer.

5. To prepare, thaw pesto in refrigerator. When ready to use, pour pesto into pasta bowl and mix in cheese. If pesto is dry, stir in additional drops of olive oil.

6. Add 1 pound of cooked pasta (preferably fettuccine) to pesto, and toss until well coated. Serve immediately.

....

Gina's Vegetable Stew

Serves 4

My best friend has been bragging about her vegetable stew for years and I'll have to admit, it's a tasty recipe. She uses a slow-cooking crockpot so that the flavors of the vegetables have ample time to mingle and mellow.

> 3 potatoes with skins, scrubbed and cut into
>   1-inch cubes
> 4 carrots, cut into 1-inch cubes
> 2 onions, cut into 1-inch cubes
> 2 tbsp. Worcestershire sauce
> 1 tbsp. soy sauce
> ⅓ cup water
> 4 cloves garlic, crushed
> 3 cloves
> 1 tbsp. cornstarch
> ½ cup frozen peas
> 1 15-oz. can plum tomatoes, partially drained
> Salt and pepper to taste

1. Set up crockpot and add potatoes, carrots, and onions (reserve peas for later). In a separate bowl, mix Worcestershire sauce, soy sauce, water, garlic, and cloves. Pour over vegetables. Cook in crockpot for 4 hours.

2. After 4 hours, remove approximately ¼ cup of juice and mix with cornstarch (to thicken the stew) and return back to

crockpot. Add peas and partially drained tomatoes. Season with salt and pepper to taste. Cook for an additional 2 hours.

3. When stew is done, place crockpot in refrigerator to cool. Pour cooled stew into freezer bag and immediately put in freezer.

4. To serve, thaw stew in refrigerator. Reheat in saucepan over low heat until warm, about 15 minutes.

● ●

S.O.S.—Getting Help

Toward the end of my pregnancy, the size of my belly drew a lot of attention and many unwanted comments. The most common, "Will you have help?" always puzzled me. "Why does everyone think I'll need help? I can handle two babies easily," I thought. I imagined two docile infants either sleeping or cooing happily. Endless diaper changes, fussing, and colic never entered my mind. Looking back, I realize that I was lost in a prenatal fantasy. Fortunately, I woke up just in time to recruit a close network of family and friends before the birth, and I strongly advise you to do the same.

From mothers-in-law to paid help, nearly all the families interviewed for this book had some form of assistance during the first two months.

> *I had someone in for three hours a day for six weeks. It was fabulous. It meant I could do other things to make myself feel satisfied. I could take a shower, look at the paper, or space out a little bit.*

Yet for some parents whose families live too far away to pitch in daily, or who simply can't afford to hire help, what options do they have? Some moms choose to hire a less expensive "mother's helper," a neighborhood teen in need of a small job after school. While the moms weren't confident in leaving their helpers alone in the house with their new babies, the sitters were able to entertain the twins for a few hours, giving moms some time off in another room.

Another alternative is to enlist the help of friends. I was blessed with three terrific friends who came over twice a week for the first two months. They did my laundry, washed dishes, cooked dinner, cuddled my kids, and offered plenty of loving support. At first I felt guilty, but I gave in to their pampering and enjoyed the indulgence. Once I got my new life under control, I pampered them a little by treating them to a special lunch at a favorite restaurant.

For some, like Kathy, asking for help was difficult:

It was very hard at first. I was a manager and I was much more comfortable being in the "I can give you help" mode than asking for help. Finally, I just started admitting to myself and other people, "This is hard for me to ask you, but I really do need help. Could you bring me a meal?"

A small footnote to my story: Three weeks after Michael and Joseph's birth, I took them shopping. As we browsed through one store, three salesclerks rushed over to admire my children. Then one clerk explained that she was due with twins at the end of the year. "Will you have help?" I asked anxiously.

Prepare Older Children

What was more important was what we did after John and David came. We already had kids, so we knew that if the twins were burped, fed, and changed that they could scream a little and that was okay. So when my older daughter Emily needed attention, we took the time together. We didn't make a huge deal about it—we just absorbed it into our lives.

With all the prenatal arrangements and ensuing excitement, older children often get lost in the shuffle. Take some time each day to spend with your other children to help them make a smooth transition, too.

Communication Is the Key

Parents with older children agree that talking on a daily basis about the arrival of the twins and what that would mean to all their lives was key to a happy outcome.

Spend Time with Other Twins

If you know of another family with twins (and these days, who doesn't?) try to arrange a play date so that your child can see and understand what a twin actually is.

Tools of the Trade

Some parents bought their older children twin dolls; others read children's books on the subject of twins. (Recommended books include: *Twice Nice*, by Wendy Smith, Minneapolis: Carolrhoda Books; *Two Dog Biscuits*, by Beverly Cleary, New York: Dell; *Twins: The Story of Multiple Birth*, by J. Cole and M. Edmondson, New York: Morrow.)

Mother's Little Helper

Let your kids get involved. Take them with you to your prenatal visits, where they'll be able to hear the fetal heartbeats. Whether you're cooking meals to freeze or deciding on nursery wallpaper, children love to help. All this hands-on assistance helps children feel investment in the arrival of their new siblings.

Do You Remember When?

Curl up on the couch and open up your child's baby book and reminisce about the day she was born. Look at her baby pictures, her first tooth, her hospital bracelet, and so on, and reassure her that you will still love and care for her after the arrival of her new siblings.

The New Baby-Sitter

If you're going to have a family friend take care of your children while you're away at the hospital, introduce the new sitter to your child now. Let them get acquainted and feel comfortable with each other.

TOP FIVE WAYS TO DEVELOP SIBLING BONDS

Helping kids make the transition from only child to older sister or brother doesn't end when the twins are born. Parents should encourage a healthy bond daily to avoid resentment among all.

1. **Stress ownership.** Explain to your kids that they're getting a set of new sisters rather than Mommy and Daddy are having babies. By stressing ownership, older children will feel like their new siblings are a gift rather than a burden.

2. **Encourage activities together.** While you shouldn't force your child to play with his new brothers, think of activities that they can all do together like reading or singing.

3. **Intervene in public.** Be prepared for lots of oohs and ahs from strangers directed at your twins. Don't let your older child feel left out. If a stranger remarks on your twins' beautiful hair, chime in with: "Yes, they get it from their older sister, Nancy."

4. **Respect privacy.** Older children often resent their younger twin siblings for invading their space. Set firm ground rules with your twins about what toys are off limits or when their older sister can't be bothered.

5. **Avoid the nanny role.** While it's tempting to use your older child as a built-in baby-sitter, or mother's helper, keep this role to a minimum — otherwise he may resent, rather than cherish, his new role as a big brother.

● ●

Taking Care of Business

During the first few months after the twins arrive, there isn't much time to take a shower let alone handle all the household paperwork. Take care of business now while you still can.

Contact La Leche and MOTC

Make contacts at La Leche and Mothers of Twins Club before the birth of your babies. Both organizations offer tips on breastfeeding and strengthening sibling relationships and give plenty of emotional support.

Set Up Diaper Service

If cloth is for you, call and set up an account with your local diaper service.

Thank You, Thank You, Thank You

Before the flood of baby gifts arrive, purchase thank-you notes, select birth announcements, and address the envelopes. And don't forget to have enough postage on hand.

Christmas in July

Don't let your older child's birthday get lost in the newborn shuffle. Look ahead four to six months to upcoming holidays and events. If necessary, go Christmas shopping now.

How Are You Feeling, Honey?

Every Friday evening right after work and with cocktails in hand, my husband and I sit on the couch for our weekly "How's it goin'" session. Whether we talk about our fears, our future goals, or simply how our days went, these discussions have kept us in tune with each other over the years. During my pregnancy, for instance, I learned about my husband's anxiety concerning supporting his growing family (not uncommon for dads-to-be) and his apprehension about becoming a first-time father. Keeping the lines of communication open during pregnancy helps to ease the stress after the babies arrive.

Choose Names

My husband and I had a hard enough time deciding on just one name, let alone two. But one thing we did both agree on—we didn't want our sons' names to be similar in any way.

Importance of Names

My fraternal boys look nothing alike, yet family members and friends who didn't see them frequently during the first year often mixed them up. It's easier for people to group twins together and see them as a unit rather than as individuals.

Giving each twin a distinct name, therefore, separates them from each other and identifies them as individual people. Dissimilar names shout out to the world, "I may be a twin, but I am unique."

Problems with Similar-Sounding Names

Choosing names like Tom and Tim or Amanda and Amy presents problems for family and friends trying to distinguish between the children. In addition, names with the same first initial will undoubtedly create problems down the road concerning recordkeeping as well as mail. Stay away from "couple" names like Bonnie and Clyde, Anthony and Cleopatra, and the like, which may seem cute at birth but will surely be resented by your children as they become adults. "Theme" names like Daisy and Iris or Hope and Charity reinforce unit thinking as well and should be avoided. Remember, your kids must live with the names that you have chosen for them, so select them wisely.

It's Almost Time

Now that your maternity "to do" list is quickly dwindling and D-day (delivery day) is rapidly approaching, make an effort to share some special time with your spouse. Do something memorable and out-of-the-ordinary, like going to the opera or dining at a very romantic restaurant. Do it now—you may not get the chance again for a long time.

•4•

The First Month:
Dirty Little Secrets
Parents Won't Tell You

I can't remember what the first month was like. We lived in a fog. A complete fog.

What are the first few months like with newborn twins? To many parents, it remains a mystery. (Sleep deprivation numbs the brain.) While that may be unsettling to expectant parents, the good news is that we all lived through it. Although the first four weeks will seem endless, try to relax and enjoy the crazy ride. Before you know it, they'll be off to college.

Developmental Milestones

What's going on inside a newborn's head? It may not seem like much as your twins peacefully lie in your arms, but during the first month of life your babies will change in many ways. Most of babies' reflexes at this early stage are instinctual, like the rooting reflex (where baby turns his head toward a specific stimulus). You'll notice the rooting reflex when babies are hungry and they frantically search for your breast. The ability to suck is also instinctual, but babies will, however, stop sucking if they hear something or if an object catches their interest. Another fascinating instinctual movement to watch for is the Moro reflex, where babies fling their arms out and then quickly retract them tightly across their chests. And those peculiar, jerking body movements are also normal and will disappear within a few months.

During the first month, babies will cry often—it's in their job description. Blame it on an immature nervous system, but don't ignore their crying, as they may be hungry or uncomfortable. Sometimes one baby's crying will set off his twin, except at night. Strangely, if one twin cries at night, it's rare that he'll wake his twin. No need to walk around the house on tiptoes during naptime, either. Newborns block out excessive stimuli by simply falling asleep. (Take advantage of it now and slip out to a restaurant with the twins.) For the next few months they'll continue to sleep in the fetal position—arms and legs tucked close to their bodies. And while it may seem logical to put each baby in his own crib, twins often quiet down sooner and sleep better when placed together in the same crib. When babies are alert—one hour for every 10—sing to them, touch them, and offer some large toys to focus on. Although babies can only focus on objects less than 12 inches away, they enjoy studying faces and can even make eye contact.

You'll be amazed at how quickly you'll notice personality differences between your babies (even with identical twins). One will be needier than the other. One might be an excellent nurser while the other may show some reluctance. But don't start labeling their behaviors now. They'll change and flip-flop with each other hundreds of times before their true personalities are set.

Remember that these are just guidelines—some babies will reach these milestones sooner, some later. If your babies were born prematurely, calculate milestones from due date, not birth date.

Keeping Your Head Above Water— First-Month Survival Tips

Like most of the parents interviewed for this book, I remember little of the first month, and what I do recall is not pretty. The night my milk came in, Kevin and I stumbled our way to the nursery at 2 A.M. so I could nurse our sons. Back then, Joseph had a difficult time latching on to my breast and wailed in frustration every time I tried to nurse him. That night, Kevin looked on helplessly as I sobbed, "He won't eat. I'm starving him!" We felt so desperate that we even tried to feed him using an eyedropper filled with my expressed milk. He was none too pleased with that arrangement either and screamed even louder. Needless to say, it was a very long night.

While you're sure to have plenty of long nights of your own to tell the grandkids about, you can make your life a little easier by following these important tips.

KEEP NOTES

Newborns nurse, poop, and pee constantly. And with twins, it's often difficult to remember who did what when. Keep a notebook in the nursery and chart when each baby has a bowel movement, when each baby was last fed (if breastfeeding, indicate from which breast she nursed), and so on. During the first few days, it's important to keep tabs on each baby's nursing and bowel habits to ensure each is getting enough milk, avoiding dehydration (see page 80, "Are My Babies Getting Enough?").

Michael & Joseph's Daily Schedule — DATE January 31

| | Joseph | | | | | | Michael | | | | |
TIME	NURSED (MINUTES)	SIDE	BM	VOID	MED/OTHER	TIME	NURSED (MINUTES)	SIDE	BM	VOID	MED/OTHER
6AM	12 min	L		✓		6:15A	15min	R		✓	
9:30	20 min	R	✓	✓		9:30	20min	L		✓	
noon	10 min	L		✓		noon	18 min	R	✓	✓	
3p	20 min	L		✓		3:20p	22 min	R		✓	
5p	10 min	R	✓	✓		5p	10 min	L			
7:30p	40 min	L		✓		7:30p	40 min	R	✓	✓	
11p	25min	R		✓		11p	25min	L		✓	
3AM	15 min	R		✓		3:15A	20 min	L	✓	✓	

TAKE CARE OF YOURSELF

You won't be able to take care of the babies properly unless you take care of yourself. Unfortunately, that sounds so much easier than it is. Eat wholesome, nourishing food, especially if you're nursing. (Now's the time to dip into the freezer for all those great meals you prepared ahead of time.) Remember, what you eat, your babies eat too. Drink at least eight glasses of liquid each day to keep up your milk supply, and don't forget to continue taking your prenatal vitamins.

SLEEP WHEN YOU CAN

New babies keep odd hours and for the first few weeks, so will you. You'll be up several times a night attending to their demands, so you'll need to catch up on your sleep during the day. Nap when the babies nap and go to bed when they do.

DON'T ANSWER THE PHONE

Right after our babies were born, we called family and friends telling them the great news, then we asked them not to call us for awhile. During the first month, phone calls were the number one annoyance. Well-meaning folks seem to have a knack for calling right when you've finally gotten the kids (and yourself) down for a nap. Until you're fully rested, don't answer the phone; let the machine get it. If you feel guilty about isolating yourself from your family, leave daily messages on your machine updating callers on the progress of your twins.

PATERNITY LEAVE

If financially possible, have your spouse take paternity leave from his job. Not only is the extra pair of hands useful, but it's a wonderful opportunity for dad to bond with his babies, too.

PRIORITIZE CHORES

If you're one of those people who need to have the bed made every day, or the bathroom sparkle, forget it. Let the housework go for a few weeks. Dust bunnies never sent anyone to the hospital. Instead, spend the time catching up on sleep and getting to know your babies. Pick and choose the chores that absolutely need to get done and leave the rest for another time—like in two years.

KEEP THINGS SIMPLE

My sister-in-law hosted a Christmas Eve dinner party *two weeks* after the birth of her daughter. She doesn't recommend it. We all have to eat and we all need some sense of order in our homes, but now is not the time to cook elaborate dinners or rearrange the guest towels in the bathroom. A bowl of spaghetti and a salad is a quick and satisfying dinner; leave the chocolate souffles for another time.

I clean my bedroom by simply pulling the comforter up over whatever is on the bed that morning. I avoid dishes by grilling fish and chicken on the outdoor grill, and I'm always concocting simple one-dish dinners. And I have been known to drink directly from the milk carton to avoid washing an extra glass!

POSTPARTUM DEPRESSION

Getting the "baby blues" immediately following childbirth is perfectly normal. What with the lack of sleep, hormonal changes, crazy hours, and total disruption to our lives, it's a wonder that we don't just skip town after the birth of our children. Keep the blues to a minimum by getting out of the house. Even infants love a change of scenery, and so will you. New moms and dads are often afraid to take their newborns out in public for fear that their babies will get sick, but as long as you stay away from enclosed spaces (like airplanes) and stuffy buildings, your babies will be fine. If you live in a cold climate, just be sure to dress your babies properly. If you have any doubts or concerns, call your pediatrician.

While the majority of women bounce back quickly following childbirth, it's important to note that for some women (about 1 in 500) postpartum depression is severe. These new moms find themselves unable to cope with the day-to-day responsibilities of family, as intense feelings of isolation and resentment for the baby begin to overcome their lives. Psychotherapy, medication, and/or hospitalization may be necessary. Therefore, depression of any kind in postpartum women should never be dismissed or ignored.

NIGHTTIME FEEDINGS AND FRIVOLITY

Nighttime is the worst time for any new parent. Problems seem to be magnified tenfold at 4 A.M. The problem lies in a scheduling conflict—many new babies experience "turnaround," where they are awake most of the night and sleep most of the day (much to the disappointment of their moms and dads). Try changing the pattern by stimulating your babies during the day with lots of playtime and an afternoon bath, then slowly winding things down around dinner in preparation for bedtime. Don't let babies take extended naps during the day either—wake them after four hours. And try to avoid naps after 4:30 P.M.

If you're bottle feeding your twins, alternate the night shift with your spouse or another member of the household so that each of you will have a full night of rest. If you're breastfeeding, consider the family bed, a practice where your babies sleep with you either together or one at a time. Many nursing women swear by the family bed. By bringing baby in bed, Mom is free to doze off while her infant nurses. Some parents, though, worry that if they invite their babies in bed with them, they'll never want to leave. Advocates of the family bed say it simply isn't so. Eventually, they reason, all children want to sleep in their own beds. But if this is a concern for you, use the family bed only during the first two months, when babies nurse frequently throughout the night, then cut out the practice before a habit is set.

CREATE BABY STATIONS

Leave plenty of diapers, wipes, and pacifiers at designated points around the house, avoiding the need to head back to the nursery every time someone needs changing.

RELY ON FAMILY AND FRIENDS

Now is not the time to be proud. New parents of twins need the help and support of their families and friends. If someone suggests cooking you a meal, accept graciously and don't feel guilty!

TELLING TWINS APART

A dark nursery. Two little bald heads. Who's who? Even parents of fraternal twins have a difficult time telling their infants apart. Try the following tips:

- Keep the hospital ankle tags on for the first few weeks until you can distinguish Baby A from Baby B.

- Color-code their clothing—Baby A wears only blue; Baby B, only yellow.

- Apply a touch of nail polish to Baby A's toe.

- Look for a distinguishing feature such as a birthmark. (During the first month, my husband used the shape of our sons' heads to help him tell them apart.)

Feeding Your Babies

Feed, burp, diaper change. Feed, burp, diaper change. A newborn nurses or drinks a bottle and has his diaper changed an average of 10 times a day. Now multiply that by two and you've got one busy life.

BREASTFEEDING

In the beginning, I hated breastfeeding the twins. I felt like a cow with huge udders. For most of the day, I would walk around my house with my shirt open since it would be only a matter of minutes before either Anthony or Julian would want another turn at the trough. My nipples were constantly sore since my kids would latch on so hard. I couldn't understand all the bonding hype that surrounds breastfeeding. To me, it was a chore, not a pleasure. But that quickly changed. I kept at it and eventually when everyone learned the drill, breastfeeding became pleasurable. It was a quiet, special time for all three of us. It gave me a chance to stroke their heads and touch their cheeks and feel the warmth of their little bodies. I reluctantly gave up nursing around 12 months and I have to admit, I miss it terribly.

Nearly 99 percent of all women are capable of breastfeeding. Initially, breastfeeding is much harder on the mother of twins than bottle feeding (that's why so many moms of multiples give it up), but once she and her babies become comfortable with the arrangement (for first-time moms, it might take a month or more), the opposite is true. Nursing, by far, is much easier than bottle feeding. Therefore, for the mother committed to nursing her children, it's important to have some kind of help at home during the first few weeks. If someone else is available to cook meals, do laundry, and keep the house in reasonable order, Mom is then free to concentrate on learning the art of breastfeeding.

Understanding Breast Milk Production

Most women can successfully breastfeed twins, even triplets. Nature has a wonderful way of rising to the challenge—the more milk your twins demand, the more milk your body will produce.

Immediately following birth, your body produces *colostrum*. A forerunner to milk, colostrum is a thin, yellowish fluid rich with infection-fighting antibodies and protein, a great benefit to new babies. But don't be surprised when you see how little colostrum your body produces at a time. No need to panic that you are starving your babies; they are born with enough food and water to survive five days!

After several days of your twins' sucking, your body will produce mature milk. You'll know that your milk has "come in" (between the second and sixth day) when your breasts begin to feel full or engorged due to the increased blood rushing to them and when you hear your babies actually swallowing while they nurse. It's important during this time to nurse frequently to ensure that your body will produce an adequate supply of milk. This is *not* the time to put your babies on a strict feeding schedule. They should nurse on demand to guarantee a successful start to your milk production. In addition, nursing mothers need extra nutrition to keep up a healthy milk supply, and while some may be anxious to lose those extra pregnancy pounds, dieting while nursing is not a good idea.

Advantages of Breast Milk

No other food is more perfect for your newborns than your breast milk.

- **Complete balance of nutrients.** Breast milk offers the ideal balance of nutrients for the first six months of life (others say it's closer to a year). Not only is breast milk easier for babies to digest than infant formula, it also protects them against infection and allergies. Breastfeeding lessens babies' constipation and colic, and they usually spit up less.

- **Promotes bonding.** The skin-to-skin contact between mother and baby helps to build a trusting relationship. This is especially important for the mother of multiples, who often has a more difficult time in bonding with two children at once. As soon as the tricks of breastfeeding are learned, most mothers find it pleasurable—a time to nuzzle and love their babies.

- **Physical benefits.** Breastfeeding helps the uterus to return to its prepregnancy shape more quickly than a woman who isn't breast-feeding. In addition, breastfeeding uses up calories, helping moms to lose weight faster.

- **Saves money.** The average family spends $120 a month on infant formula for twins. Breast milk costs nothing.

  Formula costs a fortune. My husband, Marris, was working just to feed our babies.

- **Saves time.** No bottles to sterilize, no formula to mix, no waiting while someone warms a bottle. Breast milk is always the proper temperature and never needs refrigeration.

  I remember crying at night while I stood over the stove with this big pot filled with bottles. My house was covered with bottles. Joshua and Tyler would drink a little from one, lose it somewhere, then I'd have to go to a new bottle. We'd go through 20 bottles a day. It was awful.

- **Delay of menstruation.** A mother who breastfeeds exclusively (no supplemental bottles) and often (and with twins, you will) may delay her period for many months (I held out for eleven).

Breastfeeding Twins

Nursing twins poses a challenge for new families, but with a little experimentation, mothers of multiples can enjoy the benefits that nursing offers. To keep milk production plentiful, remember to drink plenty of fluids, eat nutritiously, and nurse frequently. Also, having each baby suck at a breast simultaneously encourages the let-down reflex (the release of milk from the breast) and provides a strong stim-ulus to the body to produce more milk. Therefore, nursing twins together, at least sometimes, makes good sense.

While it's important for each baby to switch breasts periodically so that each receives proper stimulus from both directions, switching breasts also helps to prevent engorgement if babies have different sucking styles. It's not necessary, however, to switch during a single nursing session as mothers of singletons do. Instead, switch babies daily or at every other session.

Breastfeeding Techniques

- **Feeding on demand.** Breastfeeding on demand—feeding the baby who wakes up first without waking his twin—has both benefits and drawbacks for the mother who uses this technique. Although nursing each baby separately takes longer, leaving little time for much else, the rewards are great—mother and child have a special one-on-one moment together, a rarity when nurturing two infants at once.

- **Modified feedings.** When one baby wakes ready for his meal, many moms wake his sibling and nurse them together. Not only does this save time, but it helps to stimulate milk production and encourages babies to be on the same schedule.

- **Feeding variation.** While most moms who breastfeed their twins nurse them together, many have variations on this theme. Some breastfeed them together during the day, but feed on demand at night. Others nurse their babies individually at least once a day to promote bonding, but at night, use a modified feeding schedule and nurse them at the same time.

Feeding Premature Infants

Depending on the physical condition of premature twins (as well as their mother), breastfeeding is still possible. A premature infant's immature digestive system benefits greatly from his mother's milk, which is easier to digest than formula. In addition, breast milk contains the enzyme lipase, which helps break down fat, essential for an underweight baby's growth. Preemies need the infection-fighting power of their mother's milk, rich in essential enzymes and hormones.

Babies born just a few weeks early will have little difficulty breastfeeding, while severely premature infants will require a hospital feeding tube using mother's expressed milk until they are able to suck sufficiently. Talk with the nurses at the NICU to find out their specific instructions for milk expression and storage, and whether you can nurse your babies or if they'll require a feeding tube.

Breastfeeding Positions

Both babies are in the cradle position with their legs overlapping.

One baby is in the football hold, while the other is in the cradle position.

Both babies are in the football hold.

Are My Babies Getting Enough?

Many new moms fear that their new babies aren't getting enough nutrition from nursing and rush to supplement with formula. It's normal to be worried that your twins may not be getting enough milk, but before you consider supplementation, make sure it's necessary by asking yourself these questions.

- Are babies nursing eight to 12 times daily?

- Do babies nurse for at least 10 minutes each time?

- Do babies have at least six to eight wet diapers daily?

- Are babies having several bowel movements each day?

- Are babies gaining an adequate amount of weight?

- Have babies regained their birth weight by three weeks of age?

If you answer yes to these questions, perhaps your twins' crying means something other than hunger. The need to suck in a baby is very strong during the first year of life, and often an infant cries after being removed from the breast because he merely wants to linger a bit longer. Using a pacifier directly after nursing will often satisfy his need to suck and quiet him quickly.

But What If They Need Supplementation?

Sometimes a mother has a difficult time producing enough milk. Increasing the number of times she nurses daily along with boosting her fluid consumption is usually enough to augment her milk production and subsequently satisfy her babies. But sometimes due to various health reasons, a woman can't produce enough milk to feed both her babies. In this case, a woman should discuss with her pediatrician the possibility of supplementing nursing with infant formula.

It was tough on me emotionally once I experienced breast-feeding. I wanted to feed Evan and Miranda solely from the breast for as long as I could but I didn't have enough milk. In retrospect, I would recommend taking a breastfeeding class. I never did that. I just assumed that you'd stick out your breast, put the baby on, and that was that. It didn't work that way. In the hospital, I should have taken more time with the twins and made the nurses know that my desire was to get comfortable with breastfeeding. The hospital pediatricians were not very breastfeeding oriented, either. They were concerned about the twins' milk volume and not about establishing that bond between mother and children and really making the time for me to breastfeed. So I thought, "Okay, it's fine, my milk will come in when I get home and everything will be fine," but it wasn't. If only I had spent more time in the hospital learning to breastfeed, to get that comfortable feeling with it.

A mother who wants to breastfeed but supplements during the early weeks should proceed with caution—offering a bottle too soon could cause *nipple confusion* where the baby ultimately chooses the bottle over the breast. In addition, if she offers the bottle too often, her milk supply will decline and she'll be forced to switch to the bottle full time. A mother should also try to avoid alternating full days with bottle or breast, for that too will cut down on milk production. To make supplementation work, a mom should offer a complementary bottle after the evening nursing session when her milk supply is at its lowest. If her baby is still hungry, he'll take it.

Since Joshua and Tyler were so small, and not knowing exactly what they were getting from the breast, I rushed into supplementing with bottles of formula. It became harder for them to go back to my breast, so I just went straight to bottles.

Breast Pumps

Sooner or later, a nursing mom will have a need for a breast pump. Some, like me, learned to use a pump while still in the hospital, where between nursing sessions, I pumped my breasts and then gave the expressed colostrum to my newborns. Not only were they getting an extra dose of this important forerunner to milk, but by pumping, I was encouraging my breasts to build up an adequate supply of milk—an important benefit since I wanted to nurse my twins exclusively.

Breast pumps are most useful when Mom must return to work but wants to continue nursing her babies. It also offers a little freedom to new parents by allowing someone else to give babies bottles of expressed milk. A word of caution: Remember that giving your babies bottles too soon can cause nipple confusion. Introduce a bottle slowly (one per week) and only after breastfeeding has been established (after a month or so). If you have questions or concerns, contact a lactation consultant or call La Leche, an international organization dedicated to educating women on the art of breastfeeding.

Most mothers choose to rent electric pumps rather than purchasing one. There is also a special attachment that will allow you to pump both breasts at once. Not only does this save time, but pumping your breasts together stimulates the let-down reflex and encourages milk production.

TOP FIVE BREASTFEEDING BOO-BOOS

Learning how to breastfeed takes lots of practice and patience on the part of both mother and child. Avoid breastfeeding problems before they start by sidestepping these boo-boos.

1. **Not educating yourself on breastfeeding.** While breastfeeding is a natural process, it doesn't come naturally. A woman (and her child) must learn how to breastfeed. Read everything you can on breastfeeding, take a breastfeeding seminar (offered by many local hospitals), or attend a La Leche meeting for help.

2. **Not nursing frequently enough.** Newborns need to nurse every one and a half to three hours. To an exhausted new mom of twins, it may be tempting to stretch the feedings a little farther apart. But it's important to nurse frequently during the first month in order to establish a good supply of milk. If you want to breastfeed exclusively, don't put babies on a schedule until breastfeeding has been fully established.

3. **Not using good positioning.** When you're uncomfortable, fumbling with your baby, you're setting yourself up for an unpleasant experience. Find a cozy spot either on the sofa or in a rocking chair and take a moment to properly position your

baby by placing him in a cradle hold (his head resting in the crook of your right elbow). With your left hand, support your right breast using the "C" hold (four fingers below your breast, thumb on top). Never push your breast toward your baby. Instead, when his mouth is open, move him onto your breast. When he's done nursing, repeat the process on the other side with his twin.

4. **Not waiting patiently for baby to open his mouth wide enough.** The secret to breastfeeding success is proper latch-on, but a mom in a hurry often tries to put the baby to her breast before the baby is ready. Cradle baby close and tickle his lips with your nipple to encourage him to open his mouth wide. Only when he does should you pull him in to latch on. Once he's on your breast, check to see that his lips are correctly positioned—he should be sucking at least a one-inch radius around the areola. If he is sucking just your nipple or if his bottom lip is tucked in, detach him by slipping your finger inside his mouth to release his grip and start the latch-on process over again.

5. **Introducing bottles too soon.** It may be tempting to give your babies bottles of expressed milk or formula during the first month, but it may lead to nipple confusion, where your babies end up favoring the bottle and rejecting your breast in the process. Wait until breastfeeding has been correctly established (between four and six weeks) before offering your babies artificial nipples.

• •

Nursing Problems and Solutions

Just when all is going smoothly, a problem like sore nipples or a clogged duct puts the kibosh on an otherwise good time. Nearly every woman who breastfeeds experiences some sort of obstacle at one time or another. While most can alleviate the problem themselves, La Leche offers free help over the phone.

- **Sore nipples.** Sore nipples are a common occurrence during the first few months of nursing while your body is adjusting. You can relieve the pain by applying hot compresses (a damp washcloth heated in the microwave for a few seconds) to your nipples before you nurse and cold compresses (a bag of frozen vegetables) after.

- **Breast engorgement.** Full breasts are extremely uncomfortable and could lead to other nursing problems like plugged ducts. Eliminate the problem by nursing frequently before engorgement occurs. It's also important to empty the breasts completely. If babies are uninterested in helping, express (or pump) the remaining milk from your breasts.

- **Plugged ducts.** Small, hard lumps around the nipple or tender lumps near the armpit are signs of a plugged duct. Applying warm compresses 10 minutes before nursing as well as lightly massaging the infected area usually takes care of the problem in a few days. In addition, increase your fluids and nurse babies more frequently.

BOTTLE FEEDING

I bottle fed and I was a much better woman for it. For the few days that I did breastfeed, I had no idea what I was doing. I started resenting Rebecca and Susanna. Every time I heard them cry, I just cringed because I knew how much it would hurt. My husband Robert and I talked about it and decided that this was not a good way to start out. It was so nice to give a baby and a bottle to someone and not feel like I had all the responsibility on myself.

Advantages of Bottle Feeding

- **Anyone can feed the babies.** Bottle feeding helps many new families to better cope with the added stress that newborn twins bring into the household. Anyone from Dad to Grandma to a baby-sitter can take over at meal time, giving Mom a much needed break.

- **Dads can take a more active parenting role.** Some husbands report feeling left out while their wives solely take on the job of nursing the children. Bottle feeding allows dads to be more involved by sharing feeding responsibilities with their spouses.

- **Babies can go for longer periods between feedings.** A breastfed newborn usually nurses every one and a half to three hours, while a formula-fed infant averages a bottle every three to four hours.

- **Easier in public.** Many Americans still find breastfeeding in public to be distasteful, and it's not uncommon to see a nursing mother hiding in a corner or banished to a public restroom trying to nurse her baby. It's much easier at a restaurant, therefore, to give a hungry baby a bottle.

- **Easy to keep track of amount taken.** One of nursing mothers' biggest complaints is not knowing how much their babies have drunk and whether it was enough. With bottles, it's easy to note the amount of formula each baby has consumed.

- **Allows more sleep for Mom.** If Mom shares the nighttime feedings with her spouse or another member of the household, she will ultimately get more sleep.

Bottle Feeding Twins

If only the mother of twins just had an extra pair of hands, life would be a bit easier. While it is possible to bottle feed both babies at once, try to bottle feed one at a time at least once a day by distracting the less hungry baby with either a toy or pacifier. All newborns crave skin-to-skin contact with their caregivers, and bottle feeding a single baby cradled within your arms offers just that. When you do feed both at once, avoid propping their bottles. Instead, try one of the positions illustrated on page 86 and give each baby lots of eye contact and comforting words.

TOP FIVE BEDTIME STRATEGIES

When babies are finally tucked away in their cribs for the night, parents of multiples all over the world voice a collective sigh of relief. Unfortunately, some babies won't cooperate at the appointed hour, setting up the rest of the evening for a stressful battle. Here are some ideas to ease the nighttime woes.

Bottle Feeding Positions

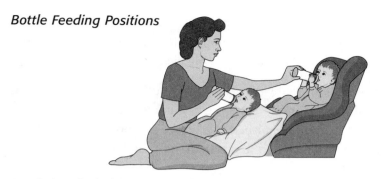

One baby sits in his car seat, while the other rests on a pillow directly in front of his twin.

With babies secured in their car seats, mom can easily feed both babies at once.

1. **Develop a routine.** Doing the same thing at the same time each evening encourages kids to respond by expecting and accepting bedtime. Whether it's bath time, story time, bedtime, or a bottle in front of the TV and then bedtime, keep the nighttime ritual calm, enjoyable, and consistent.

2. **No naps after 4 p.m.** Often, if children take late afternoon naps, they aren't tired at bedtime. Try to make naptime during the morning and midafternoon, then use the early evening for bathing and quiet playtime.

3. **The family bed.** Babies and parents sleep better when they share a bed, which reinforces feelings of security and love.

Advocates of the family bed, as it's called, say that sleeping together with your children is natural, noting that the practice dates back centuries.

4. **Variety is the spice of life.** From early infancy on, put your babies to sleep in a variety of different places—car seats, bouncer seats, port-a-cribs, strollers, your bed, their cribs. They'll quickly learn to be adaptable sleepers and you'll reap the rewards.

5. **"I want my blankie."** Encourage attachment to transitional objects like a blanket. At bedtime, offer babies their blankets as you guide them into bed. The comfort associated with the item helps children soothe themselves to sleep.

Bathing and Dressing

Bathing newborns is often a stressful event—they don't take well to water. To deal with the situation, many parents choose to bathe their babies only several times a week rather than every day. Yet others find that the bath is a relaxing time for their twins and use the ritual daily in preparation for bedtime. Other parents employ a third alternative—bathe only one baby a day.

During bath time, try using the assembly-line technique, where one parent washes the infant while the other dries and dresses him. And while one resourceful mother recruited the aid of her baby-sitter during bath days, it is possible to bathe babies solo using the kitchen sink:

- Set up two bouncer seats in the kitchen and within your sight.

- Undress both babies (keeping diapers on until you're ready to put babies into the sink) and safely strap Baby A in a bouncer seat wrapped in a warm blanket if it's chilly. Offer him a pacifier, toy, or bottle.

- Bathe, dry, and dress Baby B, then move her to the empty bouncer seat. Offer her a pacifier, toy, or bottle.

- Repeat process with Baby A.

Whichever method you choose, have all bath paraphernalia ready and organized at the start of bath time (including soap, shampoo, towels, cotton swabs, clean diapers, pajamas/play clothes) so there will be no need to scramble about while holding a cold, wet, screaming baby. (I tell you this from experience.)

As babies get older, they'll begin to enjoy bath time much more (and so will you). At 4 months, try bathing twins together in the tub. To help support their backs, sit them each in small, square laundry baskets. You can forgo the baskets when they are able to sit up on their own (around 6 months). Another time saver is to simply bathe with your babies. Just be sure to have an extra pair of hands standing by to help the twins out of the tub.

And remember, **never leave a baby unattended in the tub or kitchen sink**. It only takes a few moments for a baby to drown, even in only a few inches of water. If the doorbell rings, ignore it. Don't answer the telephone; instead let the machine get it.

When it comes to clothing your twins, save those matching sailor suits with all the buttons for a special party or photo op; for day-to-day living, stick with something simple. Cotton stretch suits are the only outfits newborns need for the first few months. The terry material and footy bottoms keep babies warm, while the front-snap enclosures make the countless diaper changes a little easier. And stretch suits are easy to launder. Nightgowns with drawstring bottoms are a nighttime alternative. Although the drawstring bottoms make diaper changes a breeze, they're often cumbersome to pull over a newborn's head.

OF SPECIAL CONCERN—BATHING AND DRESSING PREEMIES

Even the smallest stretch suit looks huge on a 4-pound preemie. If you don't want to spend the extra money on specially made clothing for your tiny packages, opt for the nightgowns with drawstrings.

Low birth weight and premature babies have a harder time regulating their body temperature. Keep them warm by dressing them in socks and knit hats, and make sure they're covered with a blanket while sitting in their bouncer seats. During bath time, keep the room draft free and promptly dry babies once they are out of the water.

The Fussy Hour—Will You Live Through It?

At the end of a long day, many adults come home from work and unwind with a cocktail. Since a baby is well under the age of 21 and can't imbibe as we do, he releases his stress by crying. Fussing (the polite term for crying) is normal and should be expected. Most new parents will tell you that dinner time—from 5 to 7 P.M.—is the most stressful period of the day and should really be called "the hell hour." Even though they've just been fed and changed, some babies still insist on howling. And when you're dealing with crying twins, the stress can sometimes be overwhelming.

Take heart—some babies never fuss. Not mine, nor anyone I know, but I've heard that they're out there. You might take some comfort in knowing that most babies begin to calm down around 3 months. Until then, read on.

FIGHTING THE FUSSY FEST

- **Predict and prepare.** If you find that your babies are most fussy just before dinner, maybe an adjustment to your schedule is needed. Perhaps nursing them during this time will help. Or, before your twins hit the wall, take them for a quick stroll around the block in the stroller. In other words, don't wait for the wailing to start before you act—it's often too late by then.

- **Tools of the trade.** Experiment with different toys to see which your babies find engaging. Try a motorized bouncer seat, soothing music, a swing, or a double snugly sack.

- **To plug or not to plug?** Any parent will tell you that a pacifier isn't called a pacifier for nothing—it works. But many parents worry that a pacifier will ruin young teeth. And who thinks a 5-year-old child sucking one is endearing? Not many. Yet, pediatricians say we shouldn't worry. During the first year of life, a baby's need to suck is so strong that many doctors recommend it and parents shouldn't discourage its use.

TOP FIVE SOOTHERS FOR FUSSY TWINS

• •

To prevent a total twin meltdown, parents must be quick on their feet and filled with plenty of entertaining ideas. Here are some favorites.

1. *When they were fussy, I kept moving them around. I had stations throughout the house—the bouncer seats in the living room, the swing in another room.*

2. *I would pick them both up and walk around. I'd put one in the snugly sack to the side and I would hold the other.*

3. *Believe it or not, the television did the trick. It was amazing. Even at 2 months it kept their attention long enough for everyone to calm down. They especially liked a videotape I had on tropical fish.*

4. *My kids loved to be naked. So when they'd start to go bananas—usually in the early evening—I'd just take off their clothes. But if you have boys, make sure you cover up the penis with a diaper cloth!*

5. *During really desperate times, I took to dancing and singing like a court jester. They didn't seem to mind my terrible voice. In fact, they usually responded with a smile and the crying would stop.*

• •

Most babies calm quickly when nestled in a sling close to mom.

Playtime

Infants may not do much, but even very young babies are like sponges, just waiting to absorb any stimuli offered to them. You won't be able to play catch with your 1-month-old twins, but they will benefit from any interaction you offer them. The trouble is that with all the diaper changing, feeding, and laundry duty that twins require, there seems to be very little time to give them intimate contact. Start the playtime process by turning everyday tasks like diaper changing into a form of play. Nibble on toes, blow raspberries on stomachs, or just gaze for a moment into their eyes. When your babies begin to ooh and ah in response to all your tenderness, answer them back. Provide some simple stimulation as well in the form of large, colorful toys.

Top Five Low-Cost Stress Reducers for Parents

Statistically, more marriages break up when twins are part of the family. With that not-so-positive fact in mind, make it a point to find time alone with your spouse away from the twins. You don't have to spend a week in Mexico to recharge your baby battery (although that would be nice); just give these suggestions a try.

1. *Every other Saturday night, my husband and I have a date. For baby-sitters, I ask my mom or a close friend to come over for a few hours. We don't have a lot of money, so our destinations are often cheap places like chain restaurants. There is only one rule: We have to get dressed up for each other. It may sound silly, but I feel it is important to look nice for him—wear a little lipstick, some perfume. And I like it when he's clean shaven and wears a dress shirt. It's nice.*

2. *On Sunday afternoons, when our boys went down for a nap, we did too. Sometimes we'd sleep, sometimes we'd talk, and on really good days, we'd fool around! We just made it a point to take some time alone and be together.*

3. *It was hard to find a baby-sitter, so when the twins were small, we'd just take them with us to a noisy local restaurant. They'd look around for awhile, but eventually all the stimulus was just too much for them and they'd fall asleep. We'd put a blanket over their infant seats to block out the light—like a birdcage— then we'd order dinner.*

4. *During the summer, we went to the drive-in a few times. It was great. The car ride would put my kids to sleep and then my husband and I would neck in the front seat.*

5. *Once a month, I swap baby-sitting time with another woman who has twins, then my husband and I go out for the evening. The following week, I baby-sit her kids.*

• •

Bonding with Twins: The Truth Versus the Myths

Many new parents feel an instant connection to their babies. From the moment they lay eyes on each other, it's love at first sight. But for others, the bond between parent and child takes more time. If complications such as an emergency cesarean arise during delivery, for instance, or if babies are born prematurely and are whisked off to NICU, a parent's prenatal fantasy of a joyful first meeting could be postponed, further complicating the bonding process.

If you don't feel instant sparks, rest assured that the feeling of parental love will ultimately prevail. Just remember that the parent-child attachment comes in all forms and everyone works on his or her own time schedule.

For some women, bonding with their twins slowly evolved, taking a few days or even weeks as the realization of motherhood gradually sank in:

I felt almost detached from both of them initially. It's strange because you always think that on the day of your children's birth you'll be filled with overwhelming emotion. While I was happy and excited, I can't say that I felt instantly connected to Anthony or Julian. They seemed like little cherubs that someone had magically deposited in my lap. They didn't feel like they were my kids. They looked nothing like me. But with each day I loved them more and more and now I can't imagine my life without them. Now I have that overwhelming feeling of love that every parent talks about.

After my C-section, I didn't get to hold Alyssa or Katelyn until a number of hours later. I just couldn't wait to get my hands on them. I was totally enamored with looking at them, but I didn't feel like they were mine yet. That probably took awhile—a few days. It was like it was too good to be true. Even though this isn't a rational thought, I kept expecting someone to come along and say, "No, I'm sorry. You can't keep them."

It took a while for me. A couple of weeks probably. You say, "Are these really mine?"

Unlike animals, who are able to bond with a group of young all at the same time, humans can bond with only one offspring at a time. For parents of multiples, this can present a temporary problem as they try to bond individually with each of their twins. "I found it took longer to bond with two than with one, only because I felt so overwhelmed by it all," one mother, who already had an older child, explained.

Twins, especially identical, look so much alike at birth that it's often difficult for mothers and fathers to separate them. It's much easier for parents, therefore, to bond with the twins together as a unit. Unit bonding eventually gives way to individual bonding as parents begin to notice the differences in their children.

Hospital-bound preemies pose a challenge to new parents as well. It's not uncommon for a recuperating mom bound to the house to fall in love with the first-home twin while the dad (usually the appointed liaison between hospital and home) feels closer to the twin still recovering in NICU. Cynthia experienced preterm labor and delivered her fraternal twins at 33 weeks. After a few weeks in NICU, her daughter came home. With newborn Maggie still in need of constant care and Cynthia herself recovering from a cesarean delivery, husband Dan took on the responsibility of tending to son Anthony, who was still in the hospital. Cynthia explains the family dynamics while Anthony was still in the hospital and once both her babies were home:

When Maggie came home, I felt like I bonded with her a lot, while my husband, who went to the hospital every day, felt like he had really bonded with Anthony. When Anthony finally came home, for the longest while he would always go to Daddy instead of me. I just felt guilty because Anthony had to go through so much. I tried to change the situation by holding him more and now they've switched. Maggie goes to Dad and Anthony comes to me.

Other parents report feeling closer to the more responsive twin, or the twin who is "easier," less fussy.

Rhonda was fussy, whereas Anna was much more responsive. It's a terrible thing to admit, but I found myself more taken by Anna. I knew I loved them both but if I had a choice of who to hold and spend time with, I wanted Anna. I had to fight that urge. I consciously tried to pick up and hold Rhonda and tried not to play into my urge to spend more time with Anna.

I found myself more drawn to my son, Evan, because he was more eager to breastfeed. My little girl, Miranda, had a hard time with it. She didn't like it; she fussed when I tried to nurse her. It was hard on me because she didn't have that eager "Give me Mom" attitude. I was concerned about evening out the attention, and when I stopped breastfeeding at 3 months, I felt that things became more equal.

When a parent admits to feeling closer to one twin, it helps to lessen the guilt often associated with it. Parents need time to feel connected to both babies, and it's perfectly natural for one twin to appeal to one parent more than another. In time, the feelings for one child will flip-flop to the other child and then flip-flop again.

Techniques to Promote Bonding

Feelings of closeness can't be manufactured or rushed. And although bonding takes time as parents get to know the new kids on the block, nature can be helped along.

During Pregnancy

Ultrasound photos can distinguish the position of each baby, helping moms and dads to recognize distinct traits in utero. Once I learned the positions of my sons, I couldn't help but notice how often Michael got hiccups, yet that annoying little habit actually helped to endear him to me. (He still gets them often to this day.)

In the Hospital

Parents should try to hold their babies as soon as possible following the birth. If Mom is too weary or drugged from delivery, Dad should step in and begin the process. Having babies room in with their mother instead of spending time in the hospital nursery allows parents 24-hour access to their twins as well. The skin-to-skin contact of breastfeeding also fosters the relationship between mother and child. And if babies are born prematurely, requiring a lengthy stay in NICU, parents should visit often and hold their twins as much as the staff will allow.

At Home

Once new parents arrive at home with their twins, the real bonding begins. Study each baby individually, looking for differences in appearance and personality. Respond to the needs of each baby separately. And use his or her name frequently. Spend time alone (even if it's just a few minutes) with each baby at some point during the day.

TOP FIVE WAYS FOR FATHERS TO BOND WITH TWINS

With so much emphasis on the mother-child relationship, fathers sometimes get overlooked. Moms have a distinct bonding advantage over dads—women carry children for 9 months and are able to breastfeed. Yet men can establish strong relationships with their twins early on by focusing their attention on getting to know their babies and following these tips.

1. **Know the drill.** While mothers generally rule the roost when it comes to issues of child rearing, fathers don't have to take a backseat role. Get to know your twins' schedule—when do they go down for naps? When do they get fed? Then jump in with assistance without being asked.

2. **It's all in your timing.** Take time off from work immediately following the delivery by using vacation time or taking advantage of the Family and Medical Leave Act passed by Congress.

3. **Play rub-a-dub-dub.** Many dads find that the nightly ritual of giving their babies a bath is a pleasant and special way to connect with their children.

4. **Allow Mom a day alone.** Whether it's a stroll through the park or a trip to the hardware store or supermarket, take the babies out for the day. Not only will your wife appreciate the time alone, but you'll develop an even greater appreciation for her job as primary caregiver.

5. **Join or start a daddy-and-me play group.** More than ever, fathers are taking an active role in their children's lives. Why not take it a step further and start a play group specifically for dads and their kids? Once a month, organize a play date at a local park, invite friends and colleagues with kids, and do what women have been doing for years—share parenting tips, offer emotional support, and just have fun.

Four Weeks and Counting

During that first month with your newborn twins, you are sure to experience a wide range of emotions, from total elation at what remarkable little beings you have created, to sheer bewilderment. This roller-coaster ride of feelings is not only natural, but it should be expected. While this period can be extremely exhausting, *it will pass*. And though it may be hard to imagine, there will come a time when you look back nostalgically and wish for those early days again.

·5·

Months 2 Through 6

I have to admit, I began to feel more confident as a mother by the second month. I finally got the knack of breastfeeding, and my husband, Don, was great at changing diapers. He could change both diapers in the middle of the night in a dark nursery in less than 5 minutes flat! Unfortunately, we were still both always exhausted and prayed for the day when Anthony and Julian would sleep through the night.

Who would have ever thought that four weeks would go by so slowly? But now that you've mastered the art of infant burping, you feel like an old pro ready to offer advice to other expectant parents. Yes, the worst is over—but a whole new set of problems has cropped up, like how will you ever manage twins now that you're home alone? And how does one person get out of the house with two babies?

Developmental Milestones

By the second month, your babies have grown more accustomed to their surroundings. They sleep less and spend more time alert and awake (that is, if someone interacts with them). Their newborn jerky movements have also subsided as they have begun to voluntarily manipulate their own bodies. As muscle tone improves, you'll marvel at all their kicking and squirming as they exercise their bodies. Their eyesight has improved, too. Your twins can focus up to 12 inches away. Watch as they follow an object or person across the room. They also take immense pleasure in staring at their hands for long periods of time and mouthing their fists. Your twins may look alike, but strong differences in personalities begin to unfold. For instance, one may be an early bird, asleep before eight in the evening and up with the sun, while the other thrives as a night owl, refusing to close his eyes until well past 9 P.M. You might even notice differences in their nursing styles. One may be a voracious eater, done in less than 10 minutes flat, while his brother may be a leisurely diner, taking his time and often slowing to a complete halt as he drifts off to sleep. As this is often the case, be sure to switch sides at each breastfeeding session, eliminating the chances for breast engorgement.

During the second month your twins will discover their own voices and begin to vocalize, often to each other, as they lie together in their crib. They love to listen to you, just as much as they enjoy listening to their own sounds, so be sure to give them plenty of verbal stimuli by talking and singing to them.

Look for more control of neck muscles in the beginning of the third month. Not only can the twins turn their heads from side to side, but when put on their stomachs they can lift their heads off the floor for a few seconds. You'll also see something you've been waiting a long time for—a smile. It's a big payback for all those sleepless nights. And speaking of sleep, depending on their weight, your babies may begin to sleep through the night (a six- or seven-hour stretch, anyway). As they interact with you more, you'll notice that their crying has diminished, too. They still won't interact with each other, but they will focus on each other for a few moments at a time, and on occasion, one twin may even reach to touch his sibling's hand. Although it might not seem like it, on some level, each knows that the other is there, and they often prove it by sleeping nestled together or by sucking on the other's fingers or toes. Perhaps they think their twin is merely an extension of themselves.

The fourth month is an important one. Your twins are no longer newborns—they have graduated to babyhood! By now they can move their heads in all directions and lift them to a 90-degree angle when lying on their stomachs. Their world is now in color, too, as their eyes are able to focus at different distances. Hand-eye coordination has improved as well. You'll notice this as they spy an object, grab it, and slowly bring it to their mouths for a taste. Now's the time to remove your dangling jewelry, away from their reach and powerful grasp. Socially, your twins are developing a sense of humor and will giggle and laugh when tickled. Now babies require lots of stimuli to keep them from getting bored and fussy.

By the fifth month, it's time to think about babyproofing as your little guys start to roll and use this new trick to get into all sorts of trouble. They can probably sit up with a little support, and love to take an upright stroll outdoors. Babies' speech is taking on new sounds, too. Lots of grunts and groans, tongue clicking, raspberries, and even pretend coughing. Listen carefully for the sound *da-da* as they learn to put vowels and consonants together. Encourage their language development by talking to your twins regularly, telling them the names of new objects.

It's the twins' half birthday by the sixth month, and already they're moving in opposite directions. Babies' new mode of transportation, crawling, usually appears in the sixth month. Whether they choose to creep with their stomachs dragging along the floor, or simply wait a month and dive right in with a traditional crawl, you'll marvel at how fast they can scoot across the room. Don't worry if one baby is more mobile than the other. It's inevitable that your twins will show significant differences in coordination. All babies fluctuate in skill level, and twins are no exception. At this stage, some babies focus on physical and motor skills like rolling and crawling, while others prefer to explore their social skills like vocalizing and interacting with the family. Before long, the lagger will catch up and maybe even pass his twin in skills.

If you haven't already done so, it's time for babies to part company and sleep in separate cribs. By month six, most babies are too big and too restless to share the same crib, but no need to put them in separate rooms—twins sleep better as roommates.

Home Alone

The in-laws have returned to New Jersey, the frozen dinners are all gone, and your spouse has just left to return to work full time. This is the first day that you're alone with the kids. As you gaze at the two little cherubs snoozing soundly in their bouncer seats, fear takes over. "What will I do if they both wake up at once?" you think. "And what if they both start to cry?" Glad you asked.

Troubleshooting

One parent plus two babies equal not enough hands. With a little planning (and a lot of patience), though, Mom or Dad can single-handedly accomplish amazing feats.

What Do You Do When Both Cry at Once?

Believe it or not, it doesn't happen often, but when it does, watch out! To the first-time mom or dad, it can be very stressful.

- **Don't panic.** Although their clenched fists, red faces, and high-pitched screams may seem like they're about to explode, their crying hurts you more than it hurts them. First, quickly assess the situation — is anyone injured? Are they hungry? Do they need changing? Are they too cold? Too hot? If not, then it's time to dig into your bag of tricks and start performing.

- **Become doubly mobile.** If singing or gently talking to your crying twins doesn't do the trick, strap them into their car seats/infant carriers and move them around the house. Usually a change of scenery is all they need to calm down. If the weather permits, go outside. Even on cold days, if babies are properly attired, the outdoors is a great relaxer. If the stroller is handy, go for a walk around the block.

- **Learn to hold them both at the same time.** It's a bit awkward to pick up two babies at once (you'll need to practice in the presence of another adult), but newborns often calm quickly when nestled near their mother. Try a single or double snugly sack or sling.

- **Take care of the squeaky wheel.** Place the less-fussy baby in a safe spot (like inside a crib or playpen) with a musical toy, then attend to the more out-of-control baby.

How Do You Put Them Both to Sleep?

First, create a sleep-inducing atmosphere by dimming the lights and lowering the volume on the television or radio. Many parents on their own put their twins to sleep in their car seats/infant carriers and rock them gently. It's safe, comfortable for babies, and allows Mom or Dad to move the sleeping infants anywhere in the house. Vibrating bouncer seats, which imitate the gentle rocking of an automobile, work miracles as well. Still, other parents strap one baby in a motorized swing and then walk the floor with the second baby nestled in a snugly sack or sling. Once babies have drifted off, the parent then moves each baby to her crib.

If you breastfeed your twins to sleep, putting both to bed by yourself is a little trickier, especially if you nurse them together. Some moms have no problem maneuvering two swaddled bundles onto a breastfeeding pillow, but I never had much luck. One of my sons would always end up rolling off and onto the bed. Instead, when I was alone, I would nurse one baby at a time. Whoever was fussier got to go first while the calmer baby patiently waited his turn nearby, content to suck on a pacifier.

How Do You Entertain Them Both?

Playtime is important, even for infants. It teaches babies about their world, and actually helps to develop their brains. Unfortunately, some parents of multiples, overwhelmed by their new responsibilities and tired to the point of exhaustion, neglect to interact with their twins as often as parents of singletons do. But their lack of socializing with their twins could have negative consequences by slowing cognitive development. Make it a point every day to engage your babies with interactive recreation. Playing with two infants at the same time is just as easy as playing with one.

- **Floor time.** Spread a blanket on the floor and place the twins side by side on their backs. Let them kick and exercise their legs and arms as you sit at their feet and give each baby eye contact and words of praise. Show them a variety of colorful stimuli like rattles and blocks.

  When they begin to get fussy from lying on their backs, turn them to their stomachs for a few minutes and watch them try to lift their heads off the floor. Not only does this offer a different perspective on their world, but it's great exercise for their developing neck muscles.

- **Cuddling.** One mom recalls, "I had only one swing because I thought if I had two, I would be too inclined to put both of them in the swings and then I wouldn't be holding them as much. I always felt that Nicole and Laura never got held enough. This way if I had only one swing, I thought, I'd always be holding one and they'd get more personal contact with me."

Parents of twins rarely feel like they give each baby enough hugs. That's why cuddle time is important. While they are still lounging on their blanket, offer one twin some visual stimuli like the toys dangling from a floor gym, or give him a colorful block to mouth while you sit nearby cuddling and talking to your other twin. After a few minutes, switch babies.

TOP FIVE WAYS TO GIVE EACH TWIN INDIVIDUALIZED ATTENTION

Finding time to give each twin one-on-one attention is a big concern for parents of multiples. But even just 5 minutes a day with one child can be special. Here's how to eke out a few precious moments during your busy day.

1. **Take your time diapering.** It may seem like an odd way to spend quality time with your baby, but during the diapering process, a parent and child often gaze deeply into each other's eyes, making a profound connection.

2. **Nap with one baby.** Not only is napping with your baby a good way to catch up on your sleep, but there's nothing more comforting than the touch of a baby's soft, warm skin and the feel of his breath against your cheek.

3. **Nurse or bottle feed just one baby at a time.** Although it saves lots of time to nurse or bottle feed both babies at once, try to feed them separately at least once a day.

4. **Take advantage of the early riser.** If one baby wakes from a nap sooner than expected, quickly whisk him out of the nursery before he wakes his sibling, then snuggle on the couch for awhile. If he's an early riser, awake with the sun, bring him into bed for some family bonding.

5. **Share weekend assignments.** During Saturday or Sunday when another parent is available, let each be responsible for one baby. Take one to the market or sit out in the garden together. During the following weekend, switch babies.

• •

PUTTING BABIES ON A SCHEDULE

Some parents cringe when they think of putting their babies on a schedule. Images of a drill sergeant with stopwatch and whistle standing over the nursery crib come to mind, and they immediately cry, "Scheduling? Too restrictive! Never!" And in some cases, they're right—some parents do go overboard in insisting that their youngsters adhere to a rigid agenda. But many parents of multiples feel that scheduling is a must to keep order during chaotic times. And for the full-time, stay-at-home parent with no outside help, it's a question of survival—put the kids on a schedule or perish.

What exactly is scheduling, anyway? Simply put, scheduling means developing a routine—doing the same thing (like feeding, putting them down for a nap, and getting them ready for bed) at the same time every day. Actually, your babies have probably been putting *you* on a schedule, but you just didn't realize it. After all, they naturally wake up around 6 A.M., nap around 9, 12, and 3, and then wind down for the day roughly at 8 P.M. The secret now is to take it one step further and slowly fine-tune their routine to better suit your household. Predictability may seem stifling for some, but parents of multiples say it helps everyone in the family to function normally.

Benefits of Scheduling

- **Gives structure to daily life.** Knowing what you will be doing at certain times of the day or week gives new parents confidence and a sense of control over their lives, something that they often long for after having twins.

  It was easier to live my life with at least my having an idea: Okay, now it's breakfast time, now it's playtime. At least I had something to do that made sense. I was learning and adjusting my schedule as we went along. It helped me to cope because I went from someone who had been working for more than 20 years to a full-time, stay-at-home mom.

- **Babies respond well.** Children crave structure in their lives. With a set routine your babies will grow to expect certain events to happen at certain times of the day, making stressful situations like bedtime much easier. Every night after their bath, my own kids toddle into the kitchen around 7:30 looking for their milk. With bottles in hand (and without any prompting), they toddle back into the nursery for story time. They're in bed by 8 with little fanfare.

- **Schedules are twin friendly.** By encouraging both babies to be on the same schedule, parents of multiples can actually find a little one-on-one time to be with each other. Just imagine what life would be like if Baby A napped at 9, 12, and 3, while Baby B napped at 11, 2, and 5—you'd never get a moment to yourself. As one double-duty mom explained, "Scheduling helps you catch up and catch your breath."

Disadvantages of Scheduling

- **Too rigid.** If one baby starts crying at 5, parents shouldn't look at the clock and say, "How can you be hungry? You're not scheduled to eat for another hour!" A schedule should not be set in stone, but rather should be used as a guide. Parents must be sensitive to their infants. If your baby cries, it usually means that she's hungry and should be fed. When a baby cries, she's not trying to manipulate — she wants something like food, a clean diaper, or just a little attention. Her needs should never go unmet.

- **Limits mobility.** As your babies get older and refuse to nap in the stroller or car, a schedule often interferes with going out. It's frustrating trying to quickly run errands and get home in time for the afternoon nap when you're concerned about the schedule.

- **Too controlling.** Some parents are so driven by their children's schedule that they put their own lives on hold.

I loved having Richard and David on a schedule, and at the same time I hated it. I craved the free, predictable time that it offered but often at the expense of seeing other family members and friends. I can remember turning down invitations to friends' houses because it would have interfered with my twins' naps or bedtime. So what if they went to bed an hour later or missed their afternoon nap every once and awhile? Looking back on it, I did that a lot and it seems silly now.

Tips for Developing a Schedule

- **Adjust slowly.** Realize that during the first few months everyone is adjusting to a new life, and if you push your 1-month-old twins to adhere to a rigid schedule, you'll just end up making everyone miserable. During the first weeks, just go with the flow, and allow your babies to have total control.

- **Let your babies guide you.** Listen and recognize your babies' cues and then work with them. If Baby A wants to nurse at 6, encourage Baby B to nurse at that time, too. If Baby B naturally falls asleep around 9 P.M., but you'd prefer her to go to bed with her sister at 8, slowly move Baby B's bedtime a few minutes every night until it matches her sister's.

- **Be flexible.** Babies are not robots. As they grow and change, so should their schedule. Things like vacation and air travel, illness, and teething can all throw your babies (and their schedule) off. During these temporary setbacks, let your babies control when they

want to eat and sleep. Once the crisis has passed, ease them back
into their routine.

Support Groups and Play Groups

For those parents who have chosen to stay home to raise their children,
feelings of loneliness and isolation that accompany this full-time job
leave many to wonder if it's truly worth it. Local clubs for parents of
multiples offer moms and dads a chance to meet other parents in the
same position (see Appendix for address and phone number of
National Organization of Mothers of Twins Clubs). They offer support, valuable information in forums, and family outings where your
twins get a chance to make friends with other twins. It's a good idea
to join MOTC before you give birth, allowing you to get practical tips
on dealing with multiples before they arrive. In addition, many clubs
sponsor annual clothing exchanges, where you can load up on baby
apparel, nursery items, and toys (a big money saver). Most clubs let you
audit several meetings before deciding if it's for you. If your area
doesn't have a twins' club, form one of your own. The national chapter of MOTC not only encourages this, but will help you get started.

Participating in a play group is another alternative for home-bound
parents looking for support. Once a week, a group of parents gather
in a local park or someone's home to share lunch and conversation
while the group's children play with one another. Growing in popu-
larity, play groups are found just about everywhere—through churches,
childbirth classes, and twin clubs. It's easy to start your own, too—just
meet another stay-at-home parent and her children every week. You
can seek out new recruits through word of mouth.

A third alternative, albeit a more costly one, is to attend a mommy-
and-me class offered through places like Gymboree and your local
YWCA. Many of these classes offer a 50 percent discount for a second
child, but often require an additional adult to participate in the class.

Going Out Alone with the Twins

*I remember going to Wal-Mart alone with Alyssa and Katelyn
for the first time. When I got there I had to unload them from
the car. I was so nervous a car was going to drive by and hit*

them! When I got inside I tried to figure out how I was going to buy anything. I didn't think about pulling a cart behind me. I just stuffed things on top of the stroller. It was a positive experience from the point of view that afterward I felt like, "Hey, I can do this."

Make no mistake—going out alone with twins during the first year can be difficult, but it is possible (and sometimes fun). Plan short, simple trips to the park or supermarket, but leave lengthy sojourns to the beach or museum for the weekends when another adult is available to lighten the load. While moms of singletons suggest getting out every day to help lessen postpartum baby blues, mothers of multiples should plan outings every other day until they feel confident in handling two infants solo. Be flexible with babies' schedule—infants sleep easily when there is lots of noise, and they love the gentle movement of a car or stroller, so there's no need to be concerned that they'll miss a nap.

Choose an appropriate stroller-friendly destination, one with a ramp or elevator, otherwise you'll need an extra set of hands to help you carry the babies. Prepare for your excursion the night before when your mind is clearer, without the distraction of your two babies. Equip your diaper bag with the following:

- Plenty of diapers, wipes, and changing pad

- A change of clothes for each baby

- Jackets and socks

- Pacifiers and rattles

- Bottles

- Plenty of burp cloths

Always restock your bag when you get home rather than packing it up on the morning of your outing when distractions are at their highest. Always keep the stroller in the trunk of your car.

As I was walking out of the Broadway department store, Joshua and Tyler both started screaming hysterically. My knees were shaking, almost buckling. I just remember panicking. I didn't know what to do. I don't remember how many strangers came

*up to me willing to help. I just grabbed both babies, left the
stroller, and started walking.*

GOING TO THE GROCERY STORE

In interviewing families for this book, I was hard pressed to find any
stay-at-home parents who took their twins grocery shopping. Instead,
they would go alone on weekends or at night. I, on the other hand,
have taken a different approach. As a full-time mother, the last place
I want to be on a Saturday or at night is at the grocery store. Those
times are reserved for my husband or for family outings. And on those
precious afternoons when I have a baby-sitter, that's *my* time put aside
for spoiling myself, not for restocking the refrigerator. Therefore, I
have always taken my kids grocery shopping.

Don't be intimidated to take your twins marketing on your own. You
can shop with two babies just as easily as you can with one—it just
takes longer. In addition, getting out with your babies is a good way to
teach them about their world.

Avoid Quick Trips

Rule number one: Take your time and never go grocery shopping if
you're in a hurry. There's no such thing as a "quick trip to the market."
If you rush, not only will you return home frazzled, vowing never to
do it again, but someone could get hurt in the parking lot or in the
store. And in the midst of your whirlwind journey, you're bound to forget half of what's on your grocery list.

Seat Assignments

"So where do you put the babies and all the groceries?" you ask. Ah,
if only more supermarkets had double shopping carts!

- **One-cart method.** With one baby securely fastened in his car
  seat/infant carrier, place him in the upper portion of the shopping
  cart (many supermarkets now have infant seats attached to their
  store carts), and use a snugly sack or sling for the other baby. Food
  items go in the main compartment of the cart.

- **Two-cart method.** If a snugly sack or sling is a strain on your back, leave both babies in their car seats/infant carriers and use two carts. Pulling one cart while pushing another takes some practice, but with a few trips, you'll be as agile as a circus acrobat.

After babies reach 6 months and can sit in the carts unaided, continue to use the two-cart method, but be sure to find carts with seat belts to prevent babies from climbing out. If your store doesn't provide carts with belts, many baby product catalogs feature portable seat belts that work just as well.

A word of caution: Never leave children unattended in your car while you search for a spare grocery cart. I often drive around the parking lot several minutes before I find a cart next to a vacant parking space. It may take longer, but it gives me peace of mind to have my children with me at all times.

A Little Help from Some Friends

While at the check-out counter, ask for assistance out to your car. It makes life easier if someone else loads the groceries into your vehicle while you concentrate on securing the kids in their car seats.

Alternatives to Shopping with Twins

For those parents who think shopping with both kids is simply out of the question, there are other alternatives.

- **Change your schedule.** As mentioned previously, many moms and dads opt to shop at night or on the weekends.

- **Take a friend.** Do you have a neighbor who needs to shop, too? Give her a lift to the store and in return she'll loan you an extra pair of hands.

- **Make it a family outing.** It may not be your idea of quality time together, but shopping as a family can be fun (especially if you stop for ice cream afterward).

- **Phone it in.** Many supermarkets offer a phone-in and delivery service, but you will have to pay for the privilege.

TOP FIVE WAYS TO DEAL WITH EXCESSIVE PUBLIC ATTENTION

• •

Twins draw everyone's attention. Their uniqueness crosses all gender, ethnic, and age lines. In the months following the birth, most parents welcome the attention that strangers shower upon their twins, but eventually the novelty wears off. And when the one hundredth person quips, "Hey, double trouble," right when both children are crying uncontrollably, many parents do all they can just to be polite. When too much attention is just too much, try these tips to get away gracefully.

1.   **See no evil, hear no evil.** Pretend not to hear a stranger's comment or question, or when you catch an inquisitive look in the corner of your eye, change directions and avoid the encounter all together.

2.   **Brevity speaks volumes.** Keep answers to strangers' questions short and to the point. When someone asks, "Are they twins?" simply smile, say yes, and keep walking.

3.   **Go incognito.** By carrying one baby in a sling or snugly sack and the other in a stroller, most people won't even realize that they are twins.

4.   **Travel in a pack.** Go shopping with a friend and spread the kids around.

5.   **Dress twins differently.** Dressing your babies in completely different outfits can sometimes throw your adoring public off the scent.

• •

TOP FIVE QUICK COMEBACKS TO ANNOYING QUESTIONS AND COMMENTS

• •

Even a well-intentioned stranger sometimes puts his foot in his mouth by asking personal questions or making tiresome comments. If you're feeling exceptionally naughty, give these comebacks a try.

1. **Comment:** "Twins? I'm sure glad they're yours and not mine!"
    Comeback: "Me too!"

2. **Question:** "Twins? How do you tell them apart?"
    Answer: "I look."

3. **Question:** "Twins? Did you have to use fertility drugs?"
    Answer: "Yes. We hired a shaman to bless us while we made love."

4. **Question:** "Twins? How do you tell them apart?"
    Answer: "We had only one twin circumcised."

5. **Question:** "Are they twins?"
    Answer: "No. He's an only child. Who's your eye doctor?"

• •

Traveling Overnight with the Twins

Sooner or later, we all have to travel overnight with our kids. Adventurous parents—those who believe having kids shouldn't tie a family down—decide to hit the road sooner than the rest of us. The secret to a successful trip with multiples, they say, isn't luck or babies' temperaments (although both help), but careful planning, a sense of humor, and a really big car.

TRAVELING BY CAR

The best way to initiate the kids to a life of traveling is to take a road trip. All children weighing less than 40 pounds must be restrained in a car seat that meets federal safety standards. Avoid seating children in the front seat of your vehicle, especially if the car is equipped with a passenger-side airbag. Recent studies have indicated that infants restrained in car seats positioned in the passenger seat equipped with an airbag run the risk of severe injury or death if the airbag deflates during an accident.

Equipment Checklist for Road Warriors

- **Port-a-crib.** Folds up and stores easily in your trunk. If your twins are younger than 6 months, they can easily share one. If you visit the in-laws often, one mom recommended buying doubles of both high chairs and port-a-cribs (she perused second-hand stores and garage sales for cheap, used ones) to keep at her relatives' homes. This way, she said, she doesn't have to tow extra baby equipment.

  If your trip includes a hotel stay, save on trunk space and leave the port-a-cribs at home. Instead, call the hotel in advance to reserve two cribs. Most hotels offer this service for free. Hotel cribs are small, so you'll need two regardless of your twins' age. And always call restaurants ahead of time to reserve two high chairs.

- **Bath mat.** Many homes and hotels use non-skid strips in their bathtubs. While these are adequate for keeping adults on their toes, they pose a slippery danger to young children. A bath mat is easy to pack and weighs next to nothing.

- **Night light.** An unfamiliar dark room at 2 A.M. spells disaster if you need to get up to attend to your babies.

- **A set of new toys.** Something new and colorful will keep little minds occupied during a long car trip (or plane ride). But dole out the goodies slowly—only one toy an hour.

TRAVELING BY PLANE

When I flew alone with my sons for the first time, I helped myself tremendously by booking three seats, one for each of us. Although the airlines would have allowed me to hold one baby on my lap, I decided against it for the sake of their safety as well as my sanity. In addition to the potential risk of holding a baby during a flight, I wouldn't have been able to attend to my other twin if he had needed me. Safety aside, one double-duty mother and father upon returning from England explained the imposition of holding both babies during a flight, "You can't eat or take a sip of coffee because each of you has a baby on your lap. You can't do anything!"

By law, everything in an aircraft must be restrained, yet babies are the exception. Although several organizations are lobbying Congress to make infant restraints mandatory on all airline flights, it's still legal for an adult to hold a child under the age of 2 on her lap.

If you're planning on taking a flight with your twins, keep in mind that if you don't book seats for them, you will need to be traveling with two adults—airlines prohibit one person from holding two babies. (But who'd want to?) Furthermore, due to the limited number of oxygen masks in each row of seats, the family may have to split up. And while the bulkhead seats offer much more leg room, great for a mini-play area for the kids once the plane is airborne, you'll have to stow your carry-on bags overhead—not always convenient when you need to quickly grab a diaper or bottle.

Other Tips to Avoid Turbulence in the Sky

- **Call the airline.** Some airlines offer additional help for families with children by providing on-board cribs that fasten to the bulkhead seats and kids' meals complete with toys. All airlines require that you bring your own car seats, and some will allow only one car seat per aisle, so be sure to ask.

- **Allow extra time.** If your kids don't slow you down, the countless bags, strollers, and car seats will. Leave yourself plenty of extra time.

- **Plan for the worst.** Stuck at the Dallas airport at 2 A.M., a friend once roamed the terminal frantically searching for diapers. She never thought that her flight would be delayed for so long and didn't pack enough disposables. Always pack twice as many diapers, bottles, and snacks as you think you'll need.

- **Travel off-peak.** If you plan on holding your twins during the flight, travel during off-peak times (midweek is best) to increase your chances of finding additional empty seats. Furthermore, book the aisle and window seats, leaving the middle seat unoccupied. Airlines often won't assign the odd middle seat unless the flight is full.

Europe and Beyond

If you've set your sights across the ocean, consider these tips.

- **ID bracelets/necklaces.** On the off chance that your children get lost in a crowded museum or park, have your kids wear ID bracelets or necklaces. On the front write the child's name and the statement "Please take me to the American Embassy or the hotel listed on the back." As you move from city to city, change the hotel address taped to the back.

- **Harnesses.** It may seem like a barbaric way to keep tabs on your kids, but a harness and leash is a safe way to control two energetic toddlers in a crowded airport or train station.

- **Umbrella strollers with clip and backpacks.** Europe isn't a stroller-friendly continent. One double-duty couple recently back from a trip to Great Britain wished they had brought along baby backpacks. "We had forgotten that many of the historic buildings don't have elevators or ramps. One of us always had to stay outside with the kids while the other ran inside to take a look."

    Two umbrella strollers with a clip (Connect Two is available from baby product catalogs; see Appendix) and two baby backpacks offer a variety of combinations to suit virtually every touring need: two single strollers; one double stroller (clip the two singles together); one stroller and one backpack; two backpacks.

Getting Out Without the Twins

With all the extra attention that new twins demand, it's no wonder the marriage is often put on hold. But the bond between husband and wife should be the more important one—without a cohesive mother-father relationship, the family unit could be in jeopardy. To keep the marriage on track, maintain open lines of communication, and most importantly, insist on time alone as a couple.

Parents don't necessarily have to leave the house, however, to spend quality time together. Some innovative husbands and wives make a date for the backyard patio (after the kids are asleep, of course). A little wine, some candlelight, a frozen dinner (who has time to cook?), and the baby monitor set the mood for intimate conversation and help to respark spousal love.

TOP FIVE WAYS TO RENEW MARITAL INTIMACY

Most couples will admit (in private anyway) that when a new baby arrives (let alone *two*), lovemaking goes out the window. But there are many ways to make your spouse feel loved and needed until that old magic feeling returns.

1. **Focus on being nice.** When the twins won't go to sleep at the appointed time, or whine the moment a family sits down to eat, in their frustration parents often lash out in anger at each other. It helps to remember that infancy is a temporary stage. Life will regain some sense of order before you know it. In the meantime, focus on being nice to each other by minding your manners. A simple "please" and "thank you" go a long way toward making someone feel appreciated and can defuse an otherwise tense situation.

2. **Indulge in simple pleasures.** Does he like Merlot? Does she have a passion for chocolate-covered strawberries? Surprise each other with little gifts that each of you finds special.

3. **Shower together.** Not only does it save water and time, but it's a sensual experience that requires no money!

4. **Meet for lunch.** Kids optional.

5. **Seal it with a kiss.** Sweet love notes or "just thinking of you" memos strategically placed in a briefcase or posted on the bathroom mirror can turn an ordinary day into a special one.

• •

Finding a Baby-Sitter

If you're lucky enough to have doting grandparents, aunts, or uncles all eager to baby-sit, you can skip this part. If you're not so fortunate, read on.

These days, baby-sitting is no longer a dollar-an-hour proposition like it was when I was a teen. While the going rate is about $5 an hour, some seasoned professionals charge up to $10 an hour. Dinner, a movie, and a sitter can set you back nearly $100, so plan your dates carefully.

Many parents are understandably reluctant to leave their young infants with a sitter, but for the sake of sanity as well as the marriage, they need to get over the fear, hire a baby-sitter, and go out for the evening. If you're hesitant about leaving your twins, ask a trusted friend to come over for a few hours instead of hiring a stranger to care for your kids. This way you can slowly get used to the idea of someone else looking after your babies. You can return your friend's act of kindness by taking her to lunch or cooking her a meal. And once you've tasted a little adult freedom, I guarantee you'll want to begin the process of finding a more permanent solution to your baby-sitting needs.

The best way to find a qualified sitter is by word of mouth. Ask your neighbors with children for recommendations, ask co-workers, or post an ad on the job board at a local college. Spread the word that you need a sitter through your local church, play group, or Mothers of Twins Club.

While most parents are happy just to find one qualified sitter, some prefer to hire two baby-sitters to care for their twins. While this is a prudent idea if your sitter is a high-school student who might feel overwhelmed by the amount of attention two infants require, it can be a costly venture. And if your plans call for an evening outing after the babies are asleep, having two sitters is usually not necessary.

After the interviewing process is complete and the references have been checked, it's time to see how your new sitter relates to your twins. Invite her over and watch how she interacts with your kids. If the chemistry is good, schedule a trial run—leave the house for a short period of time. Do your twins seem happy upon your return? If so, chances are you have a winner. Over the next few weeks, slowly build up your time away from home so that everyone has ample opportunity to adjust to the new situation.

Top Five Things Every Baby-Sitter Needs to Know About Taking Care of Twins

Found a sitter you like and trust? Great! But before you head out the door, make sure your new sitter is drilled in the basics of baby care, first aid, and the following twin-specific points.

1. **Twins' routine.** Does one child usually wake up from his nap earlier than the other and need to be removed from the nursery before he wakes his sister? Does the other need a pacifier to fall asleep? Write down your children's schedule, noting any caveats to their routine.

2. **Twins' names.** It's never easy for newcomers to learn which name goes with which baby (especially if your twins are identical). Help your sitter to easily identify each child by color-coding their clothes. Encourage her to use their names, and discourage her from referring to them as "the twins."

3. **Twins' temperaments.** Does one baby routinely cry when bedtime nears in preparation for sleep? Or does one twin have a more difficult time taking a bottle and must be coached into drinking? Explaining each baby's peculiar temperament will ease a new baby-sitter's anxiety that something is wrong with her technique.

4. **Twins' allergies.** They may look alike, but their bodies tell a different story. One baby may be allergic to regular formula and

can have only soy formula. To ensure there are no mistakes at meal time, label bottles carefully and pin a ribbon on the formula-sensitive child.

5. **Whose blankie is whose?** Even young babies have preferences. Label blankets and favorite toys until your sitter can easily identify whose is whose for herself.

• •

Is Three a Crowd? Dealing with Sibling Relationships

We've all heard stories or know of a family where the firstborn child has a difficult time adjusting to a new brother or sister. Now, just imagine that same child trying to adapt to the arrival of twins. Not only do twins garner special attention from parents, strangers, and relatives, but Mom and Dad are too tired to give the single child the attention that he needs and deserves. It isn't easy on parents either. They're drained from attending to their new babies' demands, and now their once-happy toddler has suddenly begun to act out at home and in school.

When the novelty of two new babies has worn off and the older sibling realizes that his new sisters will not be returning to the hospital, resentment can build. A young child forced out of the spotlight can resort to all sorts of attention-seeking behavior. It's not uncommon for the single child to throw tantrums or wet the bed. Often, the older sibling's behavior toward his new sisters turns passive-aggressive as he deals with his inner turmoil—he yells in the house during the twins' naptime, hides bottles of formula, or takes toys away when Mom or Dad aren't looking. His jealousy sometimes manifests itself through hitting and biting. Or when a single child sees the attention lavished on twins, he may revert back to infancy by sucking his thumb or wanting to sleep in a crib. And the closer the singleton is in age to his new siblings, usually the more acute the problem is.

It helps to realize that your older child is adjusting, too, and often lacks the tools to express his frustrations. When a child feels secure with his parents' love, he'll accept his new siblings more readily. Nurturing your relationship with your older child (or children) well before and after the twins arrive builds trust and ultimately keeps the peace within a household.

TIPS FOR NURTURING THE PARENT-CHILD RELATIONSHIP

- **Spend special time together.** Make time every day (even if it's just 10 minutes) to spend a few moments alone with your single child doing something that she has chosen.

- **Have realistic expectations.** Don't expect a hungry 2-year-old to wait patiently for dinner while you nurse the twins. He is, after all, a child too.

- **Avoid the "Mommy's little helper" role.** Let an older sibling help when she wants to and avoid making too many demands on her. Remember, small children need constant supervision—never leave children alone to attend to babies.

- **Listen.** Acknowledge his anger, sympathize with his frustration, and together come up with a solution.

- **Keep routine consistent.** The days following the birth of twins is not the time to send your older child to preschool. (She'll feel as though you are trying to get rid of her.) Make changes in her schedule months before the arrival of the twins.

- **Give special privileges.** There are perks to being the oldest, like staying up later and choosing what to have for dessert. Let your older child know that it sometimes pays to be the firstborn.

- **Protect privacy.** You may not mind if your twins pull clothes from your dresser drawers, but your 5-year-old might. Let your older child tell you what's off limits to her new siblings.

- **Give lots of love.** Plenty of hugs and kisses go a long way.

The Postpartum Body

It took me a good year to lose the weight. Even though I'm the same weight as before the boys were born, even less at times, I can't get rid of the stomach! I exercise—I'm a big walker. I walk four to five miles every day, but I can't get rid of it.

I had always been very thin. My body was never that big of a concern. So my postpartum body was overwhelming. I have an attractive husband and now a different kind of figure than I had before. I felt really sad at times. It would come over me and I would feel terrible.

It takes about a year for most of us to return to our prepregnancy weight after giving birth to twins. Unfortunately, our bodies may never look the same again—many of the parts have shifted. Where there once was a proportioned set of hips, now are love handles. But the biggest problem by far is the extra loose skin encompassing our stomachs, lovingly referred to as "twin skin." (I vow to have a tummy tuck if it isn't gone by the time I hit 40.) And although most of us have given up on the dream of wearing a thong bikini on the French Riviera, we continue to exercise and diet hoping that someday we'll at least fit into our old blue jeans.

Rising above postpregnancy hormones poses another challenge for new moms. A friend likes to tease me about my bout with the baby blues just two weeks after the birth of my boys. We were sitting together at a baby shower, no less, when I turned to her. "You know the worst part of it all," I said, tears welling up in my eyes. "There's just no going back." (At the time, it was hard to imagine that very soon I would get eight hours of uninterrupted sleep and thus begin to feel infinitely better about my new life.)

Fatigue leads to feelings of loneliness and confusion for all new parents. The negative thoughts can last a few days or weeks for some, a few months for others. Finding time alone to read or just relax is the key to rising above the negative emotions. Sometimes exercising as a family, whether it's a nightly walk through the neighborhood, hiking, or biking, also proves helpful.

*You're going through so many emotions anyway. What is
normal? I don't think I ever had a form of postpartum
depression. I was, however, absolutely astonished at how
melancholy and sentimental and weepy I became, but I couldn't
say it was related to depression. All those feelings—love and the
feeling that this is such a miracle—are all still there.*

Applause

Congratulate yourself—you successfully made it through the first six
months of twinhood. Many of the problems that plagued you in the
beginning (nighttime feedings and the 5 o'clock fussies) are just a
fuzzy memory and life seems to be settling down. But wait—the fun
is just about to begin.

•6•

Months 7 Through 12

By the time my twins hit 6 months, my husband and I had totally adjusted to our new life. It was as if Kim and Kate had lived with us for years—we couldn't imagine being without them.

Developmental Milestones

Your twins are growing so fast! And during the next six months, they will undergo fascinating changes from crawling to walking, from babbling to speaking a word or two. It's also during this stage of development that your babies will discover something even more important—each other.

Mobility is the name of the game for your active babies, so batten down the hatches. During the seventh month, your kids will find some way of getting around either by creeping or crawling, but some innovative explorers find that a succession of rolls does the trick just fine. Babies are able to sit up by themselves by now, too. But stay close by— they won't be able to keep their balance for very long.

Socially, your twins still won't actively interact with each other, but you will notice that they often crawl into the same room and play side by side. This "parallel play" will continue until the first year or so. But don't think that they're not aware of each other—they are. Twins are often comforted by their counterparts in times of trauma, like when Mom or Dad leaves the room, or at bedtime.

During the eighth month, curious little minds motivate babies to constantly be on the run. Never content to just hang out, your twins delight in crawling into every corner of the house and may even be able to pull themselves up (holding onto the furniture, of course) for a closer look at the contents on top of end tables. If you reprimand one for tugging at the lamp, his curious sidekick is sure to crawl over to investigate what the fuss is all about. At meal time, look for the pincer grasp as babies learn to coordinate their thumbs and forefingers to pick up small objects. That's not all they're figuring out either. Their little brains are busy learning how to solve simple problems, like how to crawl around large objects.

Cruising, or walking while holding onto furniture, is a big ninth month milestone and the next step toward mastering the art of walking solo. While it's amazing how far your little guys can travel by simply navigating along the furniture, their main mode of transportation is still crawling—now watch as they do it while holding objects in one hand. Those little hands have become useful tools, too. They delight in putting small objects inside larger ones, banging two articles together, or placing one toy on top of another.

As the month progresses, babies will begin to understand what is being said to them, so talk it up! Simple questions like "Where's your shoe?" often bring interesting results and occasionally the shoe itself. As independent as they are now, some babies will exhibit distress if Mom or Dad leaves the room. And as one baby cries, the other will often join in, showing a sense of sympathy. Loving reassurance to all goes a long way to calming the situation.

You'll notice by the tenth month that each twin is at a different level of motor development. One may be cruising the furniture, moments away from taking his first unaided step, while the other is content with crawling and exploring her new frontier below. Not to worry, though—all babies (including twins) develop at different rates. By the eleventh month, she'll have caught up with her comrade in crime. And when she does, look out—two tots on the move mean double trouble. When one gets into mischief, the other is sure to follow, both disobeying your disapproving comments. When you remove the item in question, their reactions will range from a guilty look to noisy rage and foot stomping. This too will pass as babies learn to control their emotions.

Your twins will be ready to "step into" their first birthday with distinct and different personalities. Independent and mobile, the babies have changed enormously since the day you first laid eyes on them twelve months ago. Your twins will continue to enjoy each other's company and parallel play throughout the day. At times you may wonder if they are aware of each other, but the next moment you notice them both laughing as they lie on top of each other. It's just the beginning of a long and special relationship.

The Exploring Twins

Once your babies are off and crawling, it can be a relief as well as a nightmare. No longer are you required to entertain your twins every waking moment; now they delight in making discoveries of their own, giving you a few moments to yourself. But many moms, including me, found this important milestone to be a huge adjustment. After all, when they were infants quietly dozing in their bouncer seats, it was easy to keep tabs on them. Once they became mobile, however, I no longer had full control over where they could go in the house or what they would do once they got there. Furthermore, there were many times when they would take off for separate rooms. While rearranging dangerous electrical cords and closing the bathroom door gave me some peace of mind, I would often scurry from room to room frantically shouting, "Where's your brother?" Many moms sympathize.

> *For as well as I had childproofed my house, I always found something where Anna and Rhonda had outwitted me. That baffled me. There's an advantage for people with a small house with twins—you can really keep your eye on them.*

When I told another mom with twins of my dilemma, she turned me on to the "supergate," eight interlocking gates that form a large and safe play area. When the guys got out of control and I was tired of running after them, I housed them in their mini-playground with a host of toys. It worked great for a few months; that is, until they discovered that if they banded together, they could push the gates over and break out. So much for that idea. It's not uncommon, I later found out, for twins to work together as coconspirators to find an escape route out of cribs, playpens—you name it.

So how do you allow your twins to explore without driving yourself mad? First, remember that no matter what you do, your babies will continue to wander and investigate, and you need to become comfortable with this important stage of development. Next, decide what's acceptable behavior and what isn't and be consistent in teaching your children the rules. For instance, standing on furniture in our house is a definite no-no (my fear is that they will fall and seriously hurt themselves), but rummaging through closets and dresser drawers is perfectly okay. Finally, find compromises that meet your kids' need to examine their new world and your need to keep them safe. Some families, for example, gate off certain rooms, either keeping their twins in or out. "I'm big on confinement," joked Marianne. "When Conner and Ryan were small, I let them play surrounded by the supergate. When they got a little bigger, I let them out but I blocked off a room or two with gates. As they grew, I opened up another room. First I let them in the family room, then I let them in the kitchen. Little by little, I'd let them into another part of the house."

Other parents insist that their house remain open territory and remove all tempting and potentially dangerous objects, thereby letting their kids roam at will. One thoughtful mom explained how she deals with wandering twins—she encourages them to follow her from room to room. When she needs to do dishes, she herds them into the kitchen and opens up a cabinet filled with plastic containers. "They stay occupied for a good 20 minutes, and I can actually get my dishes done and maybe get dinner started."

TOP FIVE LOW-COST CURES FOR MOMMY BURNOUT

With babies now on the move, it's no wonder Mom feels so tired. The first one up in the morning and the last one to bed at night, mothers of twins often forget to take care of themselves. When I asked some of these mothers, "How do you pamper yourself?" many women thought for awhile and then said they don't. Yet other mothers saw the importance of self-indulgence. As one woman put it, "If I don't pamper myself, then there's no one left to take care of the girls." Pampering suggestions from double-duty moms ranged from weekly art classes to trips to the gym to work off stress. Here are the top five.

1. *I love to get a weekly manicure. It feels like pure luxury to have someone else paint my nails, but it doesn't cost very much and the results are with me all week long.*

2. *I go to a weekly Bible study group. It renews me and makes me feel good.*

3. *I try to do something every week that's just for me. Sometimes I tell my husband that I need to finish a book that I've been dying to read. He then watches the kids for awhile.*

4. *I go to dinner and a movie once a month with my mother. It's a time to get dressed up and go relax. It's enough to get my mind and my sanity back.*

5. *I treat myself to a long, hot bubble bath. (Candles and husband are optional.)*

Babyproofing Your Home

Parents of twins have a tough job when it comes to keeping their children safe, since it's harder to keep track of two babies on the go. You may have your son within your eyesight, then suddenly you remember you haven't heard a peep from your daughter, who has quietly crawled off while you weren't looking. As you run through the house in search of the lost explorer, your son decides now is the best time to take a bite of the telephone cord. Stressful, to say the least.

Once your twins begin to crawl, all electrical cords, colorful pottery, and lamps are fair game in their curious eyes—so it's up to you to move them and create a safe and child-friendly environment. Start by taking a tour of your house baby style—on your hands and knees. From this unique perspective, potential hot spots become more obvious. Move all breakables to higher ground and be on the alert for small objects that could cause choking, as well as electrical cords and lamps within reach. Obviously, you can't make your home an adult wasteland, void of knicknacks and art. Some objects can't be moved (like books on low shelves) and babies must be taught through consistency that they are off limits to prying little hands. But remember, for all the safeguarding you may do to your home, nothing takes the place of adult supervision. Never leave your children unattended for more than a few moments. Babyproofing should never take the place of a responsible caregiver.

Childproofing Tips

- Cover sharp corners on coffee tables and fireplace hearths with padding. Move house plants out of reach and discard any that are poisonous. Secure heavy objects like televisions to prevent them from tipping over.

- Rearrange electrical cords so that babies can't tug at them. Replace electrical outlets with childproof outlet covers.

- Move babies' cribs away from draperies and miniblinds, where the potential for cord strangulation is great. Keep night light away from bedspreads, blankets, and draperies, where it could start a fire.

- Use safety latches to lock drawers and cabinets. Keep all sharp objects like tweezers, scissors, metal nail files, and pocket knives in locked drawers. Keep all over-the-counter and prescription drugs as well as household cleaners, matches, and other harmful substances in their original containers and in locked cabinets or on high shelves away from toddlers' reach.

- Install smoke alarms in each bedroom. Check them monthly and replace the batteries annually. If your home uses nonelectrical fuel (oil, gas, or coal), install a carbon monoxide detector in the hallway near the bedrooms.

- Keep the bathroom door closed when not in use. Use a non-skid rubber mat in the tub. To prevent accidental scalding, lower water heater temperature to 120 degrees or less. And remember to never leave children unattended while in the bathtub, as they can drown in just a matter of seconds.

- Finally, post phone numbers for poison control, your pediatrician, as well as the name and address of the nearest hospital on the refrigerator door. Educate yourself in first-aid basics, and take a class in CPR (cardiopulmonary resuscitation; classes are available through your local Red Cross or the American Heart Association).

SAFETY ON THE GO

While considerable time and effort should be taken in ensuring that your home is a safe haven for your babies, security while out and about is of equal importance. These days, parents need to use caution as well as common sense when traveling to either the corner store or venturing into unfamiliar territory. One parent struggling alone with two young children in a poorly lit parking lot can be overwhelming, not to mention potentially dangerous, but following a few simple rules can help keep trouble at bay.

- Use the "first out/last in" rule when moving kids in and out of the car. When you arrive at the supermarket, for example, take your kids out of the car first, strap them in their stroller or shopping carts, *then* unload your baby paraphernalia. Upon departure, unlock all necessary doors and the trunk, load your parcels into the car, *then* strap the kids into their seats. Having your children close to you as long as possible protects them in case a malevolent stranger approaches the car. And never leave your children unattended in the car while you search for or dispose of a shopping cart.

- Keep stroller or shopping cart directly next to you when getting kids in and out of the car. Never leave the stroller or shopping cart on the opposite side of the car where it is out of your sight. (When I'm busy strapping one son into his seat, I often anchor my foot on the inside of the shopping cart.)

- Invest in portable seatbelts to properly secure kids in shopping carts (available from baby product catalogs; see the Appendix). Since it's impossible to watch both babies while you shop, belting them in their respective carts prevents them from climbing out (and believe me, they'll try).

- When shopping, belt twins in separate carts. While it may be tempting to put two children in one shopping cart, it's not a good idea. If one child stands in the cart and the side is lower than his chest, he can easily tumble out.

Treating Twins as Individuals

When twins are born, parents initially bond with them as a unit, but as they spend time with their new children, Mom and Dad begin to bond with each child individually. Eventually, even parents of identical twins forget that their kids share the same biological makeup and see them as very different people as the twins display differences in personality and preferences. By focusing on these differences as well as nurturing them, parents in effect have begun to help mold their children's individuality.

Yet sometimes proud parents who want to emphasize their children's twinness refer to them collectively as "the twins," give them similar-sounding names, and continue to dress them in identical clothing throughout their toddler years. As the children get older and their differences become even more apparent, some parents discourage this for fear of breaking up the unit. By encouraging an interdependent relationship between twins, the pair has a more difficult time becoming independent adults. Yet our society highly regards independence, something that is difficult for twins to achieve when they are grouped together. Interdependent twins either remain together as adults and never marry or are miserable living apart.

While the above example is extreme, a less obvious way parents compound the unit-thinking problem is by dealing with their children collectively. Admittedly, putting twins on the same schedule is a must for most families, but the twin as an individual gets overlooked in order to save time. For example, both children are fed at the same time, perhaps when only one is hungry. They're bathed together and they go to bed at the same time.

Although establishing independence in your twins is important, you need not destroy their twinship by deliberately keeping them apart. The twin bond is an asset, a cherished friendship for life. If your children feel equally loved and cared for by you, then their individual personalities will naturally flourish.

Top Five Ways to Establish Each Child's Individuality

Although twins share the same birthday and much of the same DNA, they are two unique people and deserve to be treated as such. Parents can help their children develop a healthy sense of self with these tips.

1. **Try not to refer to your children as "the twins."** Use each child's individual name and encourage family members and friends to do the same.

2. **Focus on their differences rather than their similarities.** If one child loves music while the other prefers sports, respect their differences and nurture their preferences. Never force both children into the same hobby or sport. However, if both truly want to take piano lessons, don't persuade one to try the tuba for the sake of independence. Let them guide you.

3. **Foster privacy.** While it may not be possible to give each child his own room, allow each one to have his own space. Whether it's an assigned drawer, shelf in the closet, or a small corner in their shared bedroom, older twins need a place to call their own. Separate toys and separate books also give each child a sense of ownership, reinforcing their individuality.

4. **Assign different chores.** Doing a separate household chore from her sibling builds a child's self-esteem by giving her a chance to contribute positively (and independently) to family life. When each child finishes a task, rather than jockeying for recognition, she can take pride in her accomplishment. She will gain confidence and learn to operate more independently.

5. **Allow each child to make a choice.** From the weekend video rental to the nightly bedtime story, rather than insisting that the vote be unanimous, allow each child to make a choice of his own.

. . . .

To Dress Alike or Not to Dress Alike?

Whether to dress twins alike is a hotly debated topic among parents of twins, with each side having very strong views to back their decisions.

Reasons to Dress Twins Alike

- Shows the world that they are special.

  I always dress Joshua and Tyler alike. I just think it's cute right now. I'm not going to do it forever, only until they're 2 years old. I'm proud to have twins and I want to show them off as twins.

- Cuts down on competition and the appearance of favoritism.

  In the morning, I don't feel like fighting with them to wear different outfits. If they both want to wear purple tights, I let them. I don't care. I just want to get through the day.

  Sometimes I do dress them alike because I find in many ways it's easier to make one decision rather than two. On some psychological level, I feel that if I dress John and David alike there won't be any hurt feelings.

Reasons Not to Dress Twins Alike

- It's cheaper. As stated in Chapter 3, twins can share many of the same clothes, cutting down on expenses. If you choose to dress your twins alike, you'll have to buy a double wardrobe—an expensive undertaking. Furthermore, twins who dress in identical clothing can't take advantage of hand-me-downs from an older, same-sex singleton. And what if one twin gets his outfit dirty? Will you change *both* children so they'll continue to match?

- Stresses individuality. It's difficult enough for family and friends to tell young twins apart without having them wear the same outfit. Different clothes help relatives individualize each child and help the children to separate themselves from the title of "twin."

They're twins, not clones. To be honest, I don't think dressing them the same when they're babies will have any adverse psychological impact on them. But we have always dressed them differently because we want to set a pattern for them.

A Compromise

While some parents hold hard-and-fast rules on dressing their twins, others see it as a nonissue. With the plethora of identical outfits that many young twins receive as gifts, some parents dress twins alike simply because the clothes are there. "When they outgrow their matching outfits, I'll dress them in whatever is clean," laughed one mom.

Still, another group of parents dress their twins alike only on special occasions and holidays. "Especially when we go to places where people will notice them," confided one parent.

A third school of parents dress their twins in coordinating outfits—same style, but different colors and patterns. "This way we have the best of both worlds," said one mother. "Similar styles—like overalls and T-shirts—show off their unique twin status, but varying colors and motifs highlight their individuality."

But what about the twins themselves? How do they feel? "Our mother insisted on dressing us alike from our shoes to our hair," explained Yvette, an identical twin. "I didn't like it." Her sister Nannette agreed. "It was cute when we were younger, but as we got older, around 8 or 9, we wanted to be individuals. So when we got the same clothes, we'd try to wear them at different times."

TOP FIVE FAVORITE ACTIVITIES FOR YOUNG TWINS

Before you know it, your twins will be fighting over who gets the family car on Saturday night, but for now, they want to play with only *you*. Keeping a baby happily occupied (let alone two) is no easy feat. Rather than another round of peek-a-boo, try these fun games.

1. **"Where's Dada?"** Help teach your children the names of people and things with this simple game of questions. Look directly at your children and ask, "Where's Dada?" Wait a moment, then point to Dad and exclaim, "There he is!" In a short time, your children will begin to look or point at their father. When they do, congratulate them with kisses and cheers. Build the vocabulary list slowly and keep it short and simple: Mama, Dada, kitty cat, dog, and so on.

2. **"I'm gonna get you!"** Once your babies learn to crawl, get down on your knees and crawl after them. They'll love it. When you catch one, hug, kiss, and roll around on the rug together, then release her. Watch as she quickly crawls off with every intention of being caught again. Not only will your babies' motor skills improve, but they'll become more aware of their own bodies as well.

3. **Floor play.** Get down on your babies' level—literally—for a little interactive play that your twins direct. Be an active participant by building block towers and turning the pages of a book, but be careful not to take control—let your kids guide the agenda. Floor time helps your children grow emotionally by offering a safe place where anything goes.

4. **Singing and hand clapping.** Babies love repetitive songs such as "If You're Happy and You Know It Clap Your Hands," or "Pat-a-Cake." The rhythmical quality helps to build vocabulary and teaches simple tasks like hand clapping. In case it's been a few years, here are the words to the songs:

    If you're happy and you know it clap your hands.
    If you're happy and you know it clap your hands.
    If you're happy and you know it, then your face will surely show it.
    If you're happy and you know it clap your hands.

(additional verses: sad/dry your eyes; mad/stomp your feet;
  hungry/rub your belly)

Pat-a-cake, pat-a-cake, baker's man,
Bake me a cake as fast as you can.
Roll it, knead it, mark it with a B,
And put it in the oven for baby and me.

5. **Reading.** It's never too early to start reading to your children.
    And while reading to your babies helps them to do better once
    they hit school, trying to keep their attention for longer than 5
    seconds is a real challenge. The secret to success is to find the
    right book (Dr. Seuss Young Reader's Series is a great place to
    start), one with bright, colorful pictures and simple vocabulary.
    Keep the story short (no more than a few minutes) and give
    each of your babies a book of her own to hold while you're
    reading (try using board books—they're harder for babies to
    destroy).

Life After Infancy

The whirlwind of the first six months has come to a close, and the reality of parenting twins is slowly sinking in. For some families with older children, life as they knew it has returned, but for new parents, it's just the beginning of a changing evolution. New ground rules to the family's dynamics are being drawn up; there are changes to the family's social life (it isn't a coincidence that your new best friends just happen to have kids, too), changes to the marriage, and changes to the family's future plans.

KEEPING THE MARRIAGE ON TRACK

"After the kids came, I felt we were no longer husband and wife—we became business partners," a friend once reflected. "Our day-to-day life became a series of corporate negotiations. I'd say to John, 'If you give the kids a bath, I'll start dinner,' or, 'Why don't you put the kids to bed and I'll do the dishes and meet you on the porch in 10 minutes.'"

Raising children can be all consuming for parents. By the end of the day, they're left with little time to think about connecting spiritually with their spouses, let alone physically. And for parents of multiples, their state of exhaustion is, well, doubled.

Be it a nightly chat session, or a weekly date complete with babysitter, a husband and wife must find one-on-one time just for each other. Parents need to work on their marriage to keep the family whole. Children need and deserve a nurturing environment with both a mother and a father. By striving for a coherent and loving marriage, parents not only deepen their commitment to one another, but also set a positive example for their children to follow.

Tips to Keep the Marriage on Track

- **Voice appreciation.** We all like to feel needed and valued, but we often take each other for granted. A simple "please" or "thank you" goes a long way.

- **Concentrate on the positive.** Rather than focusing on the negatives in your marriage ("He drives me crazy when he leaves the dirty diapers in the nursery!"), reflect on the positive qualities of your mate. Is he a good father? Is she a loving mother? Is he faithful? Is she truthful? Does he love to sing to the kids?

- **Call a meeting.** If your marriage is beginning to feel more like a corporation than a spiritual union, hold a board of directors meeting. Find a quiet time each week to talk and reconnect with your spouse. Discuss issues that are troubling you or pleasing you, or simply discuss the family's future. The point of a weekly or nightly gab session is not necessarily to complain, but just to check in with each other.

The Stay-at-Home Mom

Although many dads have quit the rat race to keep the home fires burning, the majority of stay-at-home parents continue to be moms.

And while many women take to the role like a duck to water, others have feelings of inadequacy as they struggle to adjust to their new lives as full-time caregivers.

Some mothers experience feelings of guilt at having twins: "I felt like I couldn't give them what they needed because there were two of them," recalled Dawn, a stay-at-home mom. "I wasn't able to hold Hannah and Maisy as much as I wanted to—to take my time with them, look into their eyes, and talk to them—I had to hurry up because someone was always waiting."

With the added burden of trying to get two babies out the door in a timely fashion, some mothers take on a "Why bother?" attitude and seldom leave the house with their twins. The result is often feelings of isolation and resentment.

Being a mom is the hardest job you'll ever have but also the most rewarding. Make no mistake—there will be days when you are ready to pull your hair out as well as times when your heart will be filled with such elation.

Tips on Adjusting to Life as a Stay-at-Home Mom

- **Don't look back.** Never compare your life before you had kids with now. Instead, it helps to think that your life is not better or worse, just different. You may look at your friends who are DINKS (Double Income, No Kids) and feel envious as they dart off on a last-minute ski trip to Aspen, but there is truth to the old cliché, "The grass is always greener on the other side of the fence." They might be secretly wishing to start a family and be just like you!

- **Give up the Supermom role.** Rather than saying, "Never mind, I'll do it myself," delegate responsibility to your spouse and older children. If friends offer to help, take them up on it.

  I always knew that having twins would be difficult, but keeping the house clean and keeping it all together was a huge challenge. Looking back, I would have set different expectations for myself and my husband Marris—maybe give him more responsibility and try not to do so much of it myself. I was doing too much. Sometimes you just have to go to bed with the house a mess.

- **Find personal fulfillment.** Whether it's a few hours away from the family to pursue hobbies, visit friends, or take an adult education class, mothers need to take care of their inner bodies as well as their physical bodies. Take an hour every evening to sit down and write the great American novel or that Hollywood screenplay. So what if it never gets published or produced? The mental exercise of writing will be reward enough. (Writing this book was my saving grace.) Many women have taken to working at home by starting a small business to provide mental stimulation as well as extra income. Local senior centers, hospitals, or neighborhood schools are always in need of dependable volunteers.

Top Five Reasons to Quit Work and Stay at Home

Most of us grew up in households where Mom was home with us every day. But with the rise of the corporate woman during the 1970s and 1980s, many mothers headed out the door to the office. Lately, though, the pendulum is swinging back toward home and hearth again. Debating whether to stay home with your kids? Double-duty moms list their reasons why they traded in their briefcases for minivans.

1. *One of my joys on looking back on my childhood was walking out of school and seeing Mom's car there. There was that feeling of total elation, "Hey, Mom's here!"*

2. *After investigating several child-care facilities, I decided that's not how I wanted my kids to spend a third of their young lives. I gave my boss my notice soon after that and I haven't regretted it since.*

3. *Since we decided that I'd stay home with the kids, there's a lot less stress on the family.*

4. *I wanted them to be around a positive role model and to get all the attention that they deserve.*

5. *Babies are babies for such a short time; I didn't want to miss it.*

∘∘∘

TOP FIVE REASONS TO RETURN TO WORK

Not all double-duty moms stay home full time. They voice their opinions here.

1. *I truly think it's harder to stay at home with the children. I get a break by going to work. I get to be with other adults and talk about adult things. Then I can go home and be revved up to be with the kids again.*

2. *I stayed home until they were 2½. I felt that was a good amount of time—they were walking, they were talking. I went back because I wanted to. I found that I was going nuts at home. Everybody, even my husband, said my going back to work was the best thing.*

3. *I felt there really wasn't a choice. If I wanted my kids to have nice things and attend good schools, I'd have to go back to work. At this point, my husband doesn't make enough money to support a family of four.*

4. *I knew that I'd go crazy if I stayed home full time. Yet I didn't want my kids to go to day care, so my husband and I worked out our schedules so that each of us works part-time. He stays home two days a week, I stay home two days a week, and they go to the baby-sitter's one day. We are really very lucky.*

5. *I work at home but have a baby-sitter come in to watch the kids every morning. They're not allowed to disturb me, but I take breaks with them throughout the day and always eat lunch with them. It works out well.*

• •

DAD'S CHANGING ROLE

More than anything, I was worried about our finances. Hannah, Maisy, and Jamie go through juice and milk like crazy. We need to get a dairy cow and an apple grove—then we'd be set.

Upon learning that two bundles of joy are on the way, rather than thinking up names and what color to paint the nursery, fathers' thoughts often turn to money and how they need to stretch the family budget to accommodate a growing household.

When we first learned the news, I immediately started thinking about the responsibility. I was more concerned with the financial burden. When I heard the word "twins" I thought, wow, this is going to be expensive. This is going to hurt.

Many fathers of singletons feel isolated after the birth of their child as mothers turn their attention to the new baby. While some dads of twins reported feeling neglected, the majority did not. Twins, they said, pushed them into an active caregiver role—a positive addition to the families' dynamics.

A father of twins has to be more involved with his family. The mother needs help—assuming that she stays at home and he works. A man just can't pass a baby off to his wife. When there are twins, there's always one baby for each parent.

In addition, the fathers said, they developed stronger bonds with their older children. When Mom is busy nursing the twins, Dad steps in and becomes primary caregiver to his older children.

The most important thing for a father of twins is to have a flexible work schedule. He'll need to help out at home, but more importantly, he shouldn't miss out on the early years. It's great to see twins grow up together.

TOP FIVE WAYS TO ENCOURAGE PATERNAL INVOLVEMENT

When a baby's on the way, Dad's involvement is important, but when twins show up, his participation is crucial to a smooth-flowing household. Here are some ways to get every father to join in.

1. **Be active during pregnancy.** Attend birthing classes together (even if your doctor suggests a cesarean delivery), ask your wife to schedule her prenatal visits so that you can go along, and plan and decorate the nursery together.

2. **Take time off from work after the birth.** The first few weeks following a twin birth are critical for bonding with your newborns. Don't miss out. Use up your vacation time, or take advantage of the Family and Medical Leave Act passed by Congress.

3. **Don't wait to be asked to do something.** While it's true that Mom ultimately runs the baby show, get to know the routine and pitch in with diaper changes and bottle feedings. Pick a chore like bathing, and make it your nightly ritual — just you and the babies.

4. **Help with bottle feeding.** If your wife is breastfeeding, talk about the option of giving a daily bottle of expressed milk to each of your babies.

5. **Give Mom a day off.** Push her out the door on a Friday night for a much-needed break and then take over. (Finally, you get to do things your way!)

Introducing Solid Foods

Between 4 to 6 months of age (longer for premature infants), your twins will be ready to graduate to solid food (many pediatricians caution against starting sooner for fear of obesity later in life). How will you know when they are ready? According to the American Academy of Pediatrics (AAP), you should look for these signs and then speak to your doctor:

- Babies have good control over their bodies. They can sit with support and can swallow easily without gagging.

- Weigh at least 13 pounds or have doubled their weight since birth.

- Still seem hungry after 8 to 10 breastfeeding sessions daily, or 32 ounces of formula.

- Watch with great fascination as you eat.

FEEDING YOUR TWINS

Feeding twins can be just as easy as feeding one, or it can end up as a messy disaster. Although I use my sons' copycat competitiveness to my advantage at meal time, it sometimes backfires. When Joseph turns his nose up at vegetables, I ignore him and loudly praise Michael for eating his carrots. Before long, my fussy eater decides that he's starving and concludes he likes his carrots after all. Unfortunately, the reverse is also true. If Michael throws his cup, Joseph immediately follows suit. And if I dare reproach one for deliberately dropping fruit on the floor, I might as well get the broom—his brother is sure to do the same.

During your first attempts at feeding your babies, try sitting them in their car seats instead of propping them in high chairs. As they get older and can easily sit without support, move them to high chairs or tot locks.

And what about high chairs? Investing in two is expensive and takes up a lot of floor space. Some families combat this problem by buying one high chair and having babies take turns eating. This works fine during the first few months (except when both babies are irritable from hunger and both want to be fed *now*), but when babies are old enough to sit at the table with the family, someone clearly gets left out (or ends up sitting on someone's lap). Buying two tot locks (portable chairs that secure directly onto the table) is a clever alternative. Not only are they cheaper than high chairs, they don't take up valuable dining room floor space and are compact enough to take on the road.

The easiest and fastest way to feed babies is at the same time. Simply share one bowl and one spoon. Sit between them and alternately give each child a bite. While this makes a parent's job infinitely quicker than using two spoons and two bowls, babies have a greater chance of catching a cold or flu from each other since symptoms rarely show up in the first 24 hours. But however you choose to proceed, make cleanup easier by forgoing plastic under their chairs and using newspaper instead.

Eating on Their Own

Never be in a rush to introduce solid foods to your babies. Believe me, the novelty of watching their reactions to their first taste of food quickly wears off as the drudgery of wiping dried spaghetti off the walls sets in. Fortunately, most twins tire of waiting their turn to be fed and learn to feed themselves sooner than singletons. Not with forks or spoons, mind you, but they can do very nicely with finger foods, bite-sized pieces of cheese, or well-cooked nuggets of vegetables or meat. When they do show interest in using a spoon, however, encourage and praise their efforts even though most of the food will wind up on the floor instead of in their mouths. And as you scrub the kitchen floor for the third time that day, just remember, you're one step closer (albeit a messy one) to your twins' eating independently.

As they get older, you might want to move your two epicureans farther apart at the table. Once twins discover an overhand throw, they'll spend most of meal time catapulting peas at each other. Remember, too, that although they enjoy sharing meal time together, babies will often have different taste preferences. Don't get troubled when one child prefers carrots while the other insists on eating only corn. Just continue to offer a wide variety of fruits and vegetables and eventually their tastes will mature and expand. And someday, God willing, they'll even ask for a second helping of lima beans.

What a Year It's Been!

So much has happened during the past year. Not only have your twins grown from sleepy, little cherubs to active, inquisitive toddlers, but you have undoubtedly done some changing, too. After all, who can calm two babies at once quicker than you? And did you ever think you could get them both fed and dressed and out the door in time for their afternoon play date? Those are not easy feats. Now, if you can only make it through toddlerhood and the dreaded terrible twos!

∘7∘

The Toddler Years

*My husband doesn't understand why I'm so tired when I
get home from the park with the twins. He thinks I have it
easy just relaxing on the grass enjoying the sunshine.
Little does he know that I've spent the last few hours
chasing after two toddlers who think it's funny to run in
opposite directions.*

And they're off! The toddler years are a great time for families with
twins—that is, if Mom and Dad can keep up. While it's fascinating to
watch your dynamic duo develop and change, the toddler years can be
exhausting, too. Preschool twins are constantly on the go, pairing up
together to get into all kinds of mischief.

Developmental Milestones

Following your babies' first birthday, you'll struggle to keep up with
their boundless energy. In constant motion, your pair may have mastered the art of climbing, so don't be surprised if they make it out of
their cribs and into your room one night. This is also the age when
their "twinness" becomes more apparent—an enchanting time indeed.
Inseparable buddies, your kids will spend their morning chasing each
other around the yard or rolling together on the living-room floor.

Twins are amazingly sensitive to each other's needs as well. If you offer one twin a treat, he'll often give it to his sibling first before taking one for himself. They may not nap or even go to bed at night unless their counterpart is close at hand.

It's the age of imitation, too. If you reprimand one for pulling the dog's tail, beware—the other is sure to do the same. It doesn't matter that he, too, gets scolded for the deed; his copycat behavior gets him exactly what he wants—attention from you. And that's just the beginning of your toddler-times-two headaches. Twins notoriously encourage each other to push the envelope just a little further. While in the park, a 1-year-old singleton will venture only a few feet away from Mom or Dad, but twins acting together tend to be braver, sometimes wandering so far away that you'll wonder if they're ever coming back.

By 18 months, your twins can usually point to a variety of body parts when asked, and can understand simple commands. Babbling begins to take the form of true words and boy, do toddlers love using the few they know—especially with each other. You'll often overhear them in a serious but primitive conversation with one another. Are they really communicating? While some twins develop a private language that only they can understand, the chances are extremely rare. Most likely your pair is merely practicing for the time when they really can talk to each other.

Well into toddlerhood by 2 years old, many twins develop very definite roles within their relationship. You'll clearly see that one is the leader, always forging ahead into uncharted territory with the follower just steps behind. There's no need to worry that these roles are permanent, though. As your twins begin developing a sense of self over the next few years, their intertwin roles are bound to flip-flop. You'll also witness the two seesaw in their developing talents. One child may be a master articulator, bombarding you with her particular insights on the world, while your other twin may be more reserved, content to spend the morning quietly building block towers. Once again, there's no need for concern. Every individual (even twins) tends to fluctuate in his abilities throughout life.

For the typical 3-year-old, play and imagination come in many different forms, from imaginary friends to naughty phantoms who kick over the flower pots. But when preschool twins team up, they often invent award-winning tall tales. While it may seem like lying to some, exaggeration is actually a normal stage of development. When playing together, young twins also like to change their identities. No longer content with the names Jill and John, you suddenly find that you are living with Madonna and Michael Jordan. This harmless form of imaginary play often tests the patience of parents when the two refuse to come to dinner until addressed by their new names.

By age 4, your twins will begin to show more self-control. It's a welcome relief for parents as their twins learn to cooperate better and share toys with each other, but this is also the time when kids love to test boundaries, much to the chagrin of their parents. "No" becomes a preferred word, and when you double that, you may feel like it's the terrible twos all over again. By now, many twins have become more social, requesting to play with others compared to playing with just each other. "We have no one to play with," becomes a favorite rainy-day expression. Yet many twins are still content to play within their own tight-knit circle of two. While it may be easier for parents to just let the two of them play, it's important to expand their circle of friends by introducing twins to other children their own age. Not only will this help them prepare for school, but twins who play with other children develop better speech.

As Toddlers Grow—From Two Naps to One

The time will ultimately come when your young toddlers will give up a nap, and as is often the case, one child will want to do it sooner than the other. For those of us who have our twins on the same schedule, shifting to one nap a day can be more of an adjustment for us than it is for our kids. So what should parents do?

Toddlers give up a nap anywhere from 12 to 18 months. The majority give up their morning naps, but some, like mine, sleep soundly during the midmorning but refuse to go down in the afternoon. You'll know a scheduling adjustment is needed when you peek into the nursery one afternoon to find one child up and playing in his crib, while the other is snoozing soundly. If you want them both to continue on the same schedule, do you make both give up the nap? Or do you force one to lie down even though he's not tired? The answer all depends on you.

If one child still needs a short second nap in the afternoon and her sister is content to play quietly in her crib for the duration, count yourself lucky. There's nothing wrong with a little quiet time for everyone. If this is not the case, give the awake child some one-on-one time—often a rarity between twins and their parents. Let the child who needs a nap sleep while you enjoy a special hour alone with her sister. Yet a third option is to switch both children to one nap and deal with the moody consequences. The toddler who didn't get her nap usually becomes fussy at dinner or during the evening bath. Are you prepared for that? Still another alternative is to move the midmorning nap later and later each week until it becomes an afternoon nap.

Exploring the Twin Bond

Do twins really share some mystic bond? Many of us imagine that they do. Are the minds of twins somehow wired together in utero or is this "psychic connection" manufactured by those of us who insist that twins be clones, exact body and soul images of each other? Identical twins share 100 percent of the same DNA, so many similarities in behavior and idiosyncracies are inborn. But identicals are only one third of the twin population. What about fraternal twins who only share 50 percent of their genes at most? Two siblings merely sharing the same birthday have their twinship thrust upon them. Comparisons are made between the two, however unfairly, simply because they share the title of "twin." Through common experiences, though, even they develop a bond that two siblings of different ages rarely achieve. Perhaps they are not as tightly knit as their identical counterparts, but the fraternal friendship can be strong nonetheless.

Perhaps the sibling connection begins in utero. Always fighting for space, twins have a prenatal experience that is vastly different than that of a singleton. Through ultrasound, doctors have observed twins fighting—one twin literally punching the other—as well as kissing and hugging. Competing or cooperating—two heads of the twin coin. Sacred and mysterious, the twin bond may never be fully deciphered, but as parents of twins we will continue to observe our children and try to explain the unexplainable.

Nature Versus Nurture Theory

Can the twin bond still exist if twins are reared apart, each growing up in profoundly different circumstances? When identical twins, who are genetic clones, are separated at birth, the nature/nurture theory is seriously put to the test, and we are forced to ask ourselves: Are we a product of our genetic makeup or of our environments?

Take the example of Jim Lewis and Jim Springer, identical twins separated at birth and reunited after 39 years at the now famous University of Minnesota's Center for Twin and Adoption Research. After extensive questioning and probing from the center's founder, Dr. Thomas J. Bouchard, and his colleagues, it was discovered that each of the Jims had been married twice (both had been married first to women named Linda, then to women named Betty), had vacationed on the same beach in Florida, and had named their firstborn child James Alan. Not only did they look profoundly alike as most identicals do, but many of their mannerisms were eerily similar. Both were nail biters, liked Miller Lite beer, smoked Salem cigarettes, and had worked part-time in law enforcement.

Then there was the case of Barbara Herbert and Daphne Goodship, another set of identicals who were separated at birth and reared in different British families. When they finally met after more than 30 years, their similarities were striking. Both had left school at 14, worked in local government, had tinted their hair auburn when young, couldn't stand the sight of blood, and had a touch of vertigo. Each had had a miscarriage during the same month and then subsequently went on to give birth to two boys and a girl. At the center, both were found to have an IQ only a point apart, the same allergies, and thyroid problems.

Coincidence? Perhaps. Or is it something more? Do our genes really control our destinies and thus our connections to those around us? And if so, is it any wonder then when identical twins often finish each other's sentences or have premonitions about the fate of their twin?

My girls started Irish dancing seven months ago. They're incredibly in sync with each other—their dancing is impeccably

the same. No amount of practicing with someone else would
ever make them as in sync.

It's eerie sometimes. Our voices are so similar that when Rob
leaves me a message on my answering machine, sometimes I
jump when I hear it because I don't remember leaving myself
a message.

The Beginning Bond

Although twins, fraternal or identical, rarely interact during their first
year of life, we wait anxiously for them to connect as twins and notice
each other for the first time. One family caught the exciting moment
on video when their twins were only 4 months old. "They were side
by side looking at each other," explained Kathy. "Then suddenly, one
reached out and grabbed the other one's hand. It was very special." On
rare occasions, though, parents describe a much earlier twin connection, one that we all imagine twins share:

Becky was born with an ingrown toenail and when the doctor
had to remove it, Suzie was on the table next to her. Even
before Becky started feeling the pain from the procedure, Suzie
started screaming. It was as if she felt the pain, too. It gave us
shivers — it was awesome.

Parents describe how during the first year, physical interaction
between twins is usually limited to brief moments of discovery. (It's
important to note that singletons don't actively play with other children
during their first year either.) Twins may giggle in unison while lying
in a crib together, or once they learn to crawl, they may momentarily
chase each other around the nursery, but the majority of interaction
or twin bonding parents report is subtle.

It was fascinating to watch them. On the one hand, it was as if
they didn't even realize that the other existed — they rarely
looked at each other, and if Anthony was in the way of Julian,
he would crawl right over him. Yet, it was rare when they would
crawl off to separate rooms. They always stuck together. I would
always find them in the same room, often playing back to back.
It was as if they thought that their twin was a part of them.

*Nannette and Yvette slept in the same crib for the first year and
a half. We'd try to put them to sleep on separate sides of the
crib, but they'd always make their way to one side of the crib
and cuddle. They still like to sleep together!*

Following the first year, twin toddlers move from parallel play to
actively interacting with each other. The duo often develops a love-
hate relationship. "One minute they're both crying as they fight over
the same toy," claimed one mother. "Then the next they're laughing
as they chase each other around the backyard." Parents of twins often
become disappointed when their twins fight when they wouldn't think
twice if two different-aged siblings engaged in a confrontation. All
children within a family fight; it's just that twins and their relationship
with each other are more closely scrutinized by those around them.

Even with all the in-house fighting, though, parents report
moments of concern and cooperation between the pair as their twin
toddlers freely give each other juice cups or cookies. In my house, it's
not unusual for one son to pick up two toys and then spend several
minutes searching for his brother just to hand him one. No two same-
aged toddlers that I've ever seen have such moments of cooperation.

*I often wonder how much my sons understand about their
relationship. Even though they're fraternal, my sons' bond is
very strong. The older twin, Conner, is very protective of Ryan.
For instance, if I reprimand Ryan, Conner will come over and
hit me if he thinks I was being unfair to his brother. Conner is
like a mother to Ryan.*

*As they were growing up, anytime that they were together they
had to be sitting next to each other and somehow they had to be
touching. They would touch each other's hands, play with each
other's hair. They always had to be physically touching.*

With each passing month, growing twins tend to gravitate closer to
each other—the cornerstone of a unique and special relationship.
During the early years, preschool twins—whether fighting or hugging—spend more time with each other than anyone else (including
Mom or Dad). And while it's a relief for tired parents when twins play
with each other on a daily basis, it's this type of forced bond, experts

say, that's troubling—for many twins miss out on the relationship with their parents that they would have naturally cultivated if they had been born a single child. Therefore, it's important not only to nurture the twin bond, but also to nurture the parent-child relationship by finding time alone with each child every day.

Should You Separate Twins for a Day?

Even if it's just running errands, they like their one-on-one time, and I do, too. It's a time when you just hold one hand, not everybody's.

Some parents insist that taking just one twin to the store and leaving his sister behind with another adult offers special one-on-one time for each child (assuming that the other parent is at home caring for the one left behind). In addition, the child "out on the town" gets to shed his twin title for the day as the spotlight shines solely on him. When a child is separated from his twin, some parents reason, he feels more independent and nurtures his own individuality.

It's really hard for me to separate them, but I think it's important for them to have a little time away from each other to get a feel for what it's like to be alone.

Yet other mothers and fathers of toddlers have temporarily given up on the idea, saying it's just too difficult to arrange at this early age. Before long, they contend, their twins will spend plenty of time apart. For now, if they want to be together, why not let them?

In the beginning I thought "We have to separate them. It's important that we try to spend time alone with each one." It sounds great, but it just hasn't worked out for us. Whenever I say, "Laura, would you like to go with Daddy to the grocery store?" Nicole of course wants to go along, too. Then a fight ensues. I don't want my husband and Laura to sneak out and leave Nicole behind—that seems deceptive.

Others sympathize:

Separating them always backfires. They put up such a fuss when one leaves the other. Whoever stays at home just cries the whole time.

Even parents who each take a child out for the day, eliminating the "toddler left behind" problem, find that this doesn't always keep the peace.

In the past, separating them had always failed, but we thought it was important to try again. One time we decided that John would take Richard to the supermarket and I would take David to the department store, but the kids still fought over who would get to go with Daddy. After that, we cooled the "day away" therapy for awhile. But now that they're in school, it's a lot easier to take just one on an errand and leave the other at home.

But if you feel strongly about separating your twins for the day, take the advice of those who have been there: If you start the process when babies are young and do it often, your twins will accept the practice as commonplace, eliminating many a teary scene.

Speech Development

There's nothing sweeter than hearing the words "Mama" and "Dada" spoken for the first time. But did you know that toddlers around the world babble in the same way? It's not until parents hear words in their particular languages and then encourage their children to repeat those certain sounds that babies make the connection that the words they are babbling actually have meaning.

How Language Begins

He may not say much, but an infant from the moment he's born studies the way his parents communicate. As Mom and Dad raise and lower the pitch of their voices, or speak louder or softer to express varying emotions, baby is listening intently, storing the information until he can use it successfully.

Around 4 months of age, a baby begins "cooing," dropping and raising his voice and vocalizing open vowel sounds like "ooohhh" and "aahhh." The consonants B, D, M, and P follow next as baby babbles "Mama" and "Dada" for the first time. Then by 6 months, he makes the connection that "Da-da" corresponds to that guy with the moustache who's been giving him a bath every night. Baby now knows that words have meaning and he actually responds to his own name when called.

The First Words

Soon after her first birthday, a baby speaks her first words. During this *holophrastic* period, when one word represents entire sentences, baby's pronunciation may not be exact. "Kiki" for kitty cat and "nana" for banana isn't perfect English, but baby will be consistent when referring to a particular object. The *telegraphic* phase, or two-word sentences, begins during baby's second year. Her speech at this time is similar to a telegram (hence the name telegraphic)—baby uses only the important words in a sentence, leaving unimportant ones out. "Bye-bye Dada" and "Baby done" may be simple, but these endearing words speak volumes.

As a child participates in family life, she begins to understand that all social situations have "scripts," and soon she pairs the scripts with the language she hears, thus learning the meanings of expressions. By conversing with adults and participating in the community around them, most preschool children have learned to use grammar and how to use language to accomplish communicative tasks.

Tips to Aid Language Development

- Look each child directly in the eyes when speaking to him.

- Show your children picture books or family photos and tell them the names of things and people.

- Use the opportunities during bath time, meal time, and diaper changes to talk to your babies. Tell them what you're doing. Even though they can't answer, ask them questions. It not only builds vocabulary, but it teaches them about interactive conversation.

- Sing simple, rhythmic songs.

- Introduce your twins to sign language. Some speech experts feel that infants have an instinctual need to communicate, and that teaching babies to sign enhances their conversation skills, lessening children's communication frustration. (To learn more, check out *Toddler Talk: The First Signs of Intelligent Life* by Joseph Garcia, Washington, DC: Stratton Kehl Publications; and *How to Talk with Your Baby Before Your Baby Can Talk* by Linda Acredolo and Susan Goodwyn, Lincolnwood, IL: Contemporary Books.)

Speech Difficulties in Twins

Sometimes twins have a more difficult time developing proper speech than the average child, due in large part to a lack of verbal involvement by their exhausted parents. Twins also spend a large portion of the day with each other, modeling each other's poor articulation (another reason to expose twins to other peers). In some situations, one twin will become the representative for the pair, while the other stands quietly by, content to let her twin answer for her. Identicals suffer most from poor speech habits since many times they act intuitively, requiring only a grunt to communicate their needs to each other. And in rare cases, some twins develop their own private language called *idioglossia*, where signs, words, and expressions are known only to the pair. While this is highly unusual, twins' speech acquisition can be delayed compared to that of a singleton not for lack of cognitive development, but rather from the unique family situation in which twins find themselves. (It is important to note that singletons, too, are affected by some of these factors and can also develop speech problems. Twins, however, are just more prone to them.)

In a published study of two 5-year-old twins ("Something 'Very' Happens: Language Acquisition in Early Childhood" by Glenda Shopen and Tim Shopen; *Australian Journal of Early Childhood*, March 1995), Jeremy and David suffered from significant speech delay. By the time the boys were 5½ years old, they still had tremendous trouble using correct grammar and sentence construction, and were slow in developing vocabulary—all tasks usually mastered by 3-year-old children.

Jeremy said, "Daddy, did you went for a run?"
David said, "Did Cinderella runned away?"

They also had difficulty with verbs and used a lot of non-standard grammar.

David said, "I leaved it in the hall."
Jeremy said, "We bringed it," and "I thought I knowed him."

Unlike many twins with speech delay, Jeremy and David's family interacted often with the boys, giving them constant language input. So what went wrong? According to the study, while singletons are motivated to use language as soon as they are capable, twins manage to participate within their families successfully without language. Jeremy and David understood what adults were saying to them; in fact, they were going through the same process of language development as other children, but they were just not motivated to use language to communicate their needs. Instead, the pair used gestures and vocalization with certain intonations to make themselves understood. They also spent the majority of their time with each other, imitating each other's poor grammatical structure. But it was the boys' unique cultural experience that influenced their speech the most—by spending so much time together, they became so familiar with the activities in which they were involved, they didn't see the significance of language the way that singletons do.

But speech experts are quick to assure parents that as long as twins are exposed to other children and a variety of people in general, there is no real cause for concern. And while most speech problems resolve themselves by kindergarten, parents should take an active role early on and encourage good speech habits.

Tips to Avoid Twin-Speech Problems

- Insist that each child speaks for herself, applauding her efforts at communicating; never allow one child to become the spokesperson of the group.

- Never interrupt a child who is speaking to correct his pronunciation. Instead, when he is finished, model the words correctly. "You said you like the dog? I do, too."

- Continue to read out loud to your children and provide lots of imaginary play using dolls and hand puppets.

- Frequently repeat important words and phrases.

- Don't act instinctively to all of your children's needs; allow them to vocalize their desires.

- Allow your twins to play with other children and expose them to other adults.

The Terrible Twos—Are They So Terrible?

Times two. By the time my guys were 15 months old, they began to wear me down daily. With two strong wills and separate, distinct opinions, Michael and Joseph decided to test the limits a bit early.

A QUESTION OF DISCIPLINE

Twins can think up all kinds of mischief, and if it's true that there's strength in numbers, parents had better be on their toes. They say twin toddlers hear the word "no" more often than the average child. Think about it—a twin hears "no" when it's spoken directly to him, he hears it when it's meant for his counterpart, and he also hears it when it's focused on the pair. With this in mind, it's no wonder that twins have a more difficult time internalizing house rules—they develop an immunity to "no" early on.

In the eyes of twins, "no" can lose its meaning very quickly. Therefore, the word should be used judiciously, and parents should choose alternate phrases instead. "Don't do that" and "Stay away from there" are effective alternatives. A reprimand, such as "Don't hit the kitty," should be followed with a better option of what to do: "Be nice to the kitty. Give her a kiss." Then loudly praise the good deed.

Although disciplining twins should follow the same rules as disciplining a singleton (setting limits, consistency, and so on), it is more difficult to discipline two toddlers at once. When two little tykes are fleeing the scene of a crime in opposite directions, it's often difficult to pinpoint the culprit. If neither child confesses to the misconduct, do you punish both? What if you suspect one child is taking the blame for her brother, but you can't be sure? Then what do you do? And when you do finally nab one in the act, the close bond that twins often share sometimes makes it difficult to punish the offender—the "innocent party" may comfort the "guilty party," making the parent out to be the bad guy. Or, if both are punished, they may blame each other, only to exasperate an already stressful situation.

Short of sending them off to military school until their 18th birthday, there are ways to deal effectively with twin discipline.

- Reprimand the wrongdoer (or doers) in private to avoid embarrassing one twin in front of the other.

- Time-outs should be in separate rooms to prevent one twin from entertaining the other.

- Give more attention to the good behavior with positive reinforcement in the form of praise and lots of hugs.

- Suggest a positive alternate behavior to an inappropriate one.

- Never punish both unless you've witnessed both misbehaving. Questioning both children separately and privately often gets to the heart of the matter, illuminating the true wrongdoer.

- Separate them. Even if for only a minute, separating sparring twins gives everyone a chance to cool off.

- Set a good example. Learning to share is a difficult concept for children under the age of 2. Help them learn to take turns by eagerly sharing your "toys" with them. Let them see you share with other adults in your household.

- React to each child's behavior individually, not as a group.

- If you accidentally accuse the wrong child, apologize.

TOP FIVE WAYS TO CALM
OUT-OF-CONTROL TWINS

At times, you may wonder who really runs the show—you or your 2-year-old twins. When these alter egos get together to let the good times roll, things can get out of hand. Try these suggestions to calm the storm.

1. *When my guys are bouncing off the walls, it simply means that they are bored. Now when things get crazy inside, I open the back door and let them go outside. I've gated off a large area for them to play in and I carefully monitor their whereabouts from the kitchen. They're happy playing with each other and I actually have a moment of peace.*

2. *Some days I just can't take it when each twin is whining and pulling on my pants. I can calm things down by putting them in the same crib with a few toys. They love it. Within a few minutes, I'll hear them giggling and snuggling with their blankets.*

3. *I discovered that my kids love to watch videos of themselves. They're mesmerized by it and they cool down immediately.*

4. *Anytime that they'd fight with each other, I'd give them time-outs together. I'd make them stand in the corner and hug each other. It worked. They couldn't last for more than two minutes before they were kissing and hugging each other. It made them make up with each other without my having to force them.*

5. *I use a pair of secret backup toys as my defense. When my girls get out of hand, I make a big fuss over the toys that have been hidden for just such an occasion. The girls quiet down as I take the toys out, and before long they are engrossed in imaginary play.*

Fighting Between Twins

In the early years, fighting between twins is a daily occurrence and a strain on parents, who are forced to mediate. While twins rarely want to intentionally inflict physical harm on each other, they do often resort to biting, kicking, and pushing out of frustration. They don't realize that their fighting could have adverse effects. It's important that twins learn how to settle their own squabbles, but it will take patience and consistent teaching of the rules from parents.

Rather than taking an authoritative role when mediating intertwin fighting, psychologists Judy Hagedorn and Janet Kizziar (identical twin sisters themselves) in their book *Gemini: The Psychology and Phenomena of Twins*, suggest parents not get involved in their children's squabbles (at least not right away). They should detach themselves from the situation and instead become clarifiers and amplifiers. Instead of moralizing the behavior ("It's not nice to hit your brother!") or threatening the action with punishment ("If you hit him one more time . . . "), parents should clarify and confront:

Parent: John, Paul said you bit him.
John: But he hit me first.
Parent: Paul, John said he bit you because you hit him first.
Paul: I hit him because he took my truck.
John: I took your truck because you weren't home.

Eventually, the children will talk directly to each other, bypassing the parent and often settling their own disagreements.

Tips to Ease Fighting Between Twins

- Do not intervene right away. Constant rescuing won't teach kids how to deal with conflicts on their own. Instead, observe from a distance to determine if the injured party is actually the instigator. Can the real victim deal effectively with his aggressive sibling by resisting or simply moving on to something else? If so, keep your distance.

- Never allow hitting, biting, or kicking. Immediately remove the offending party from the room and then comfort the injured party. Separation is the best way to teach a child that certain behavior is not acceptable.

- If twins fight over a toy, give the toy a time-out and suggest alternative toys.

- Twins successfully share smaller toys like puzzles, but large toys like tricycles and dolls pose a problem. It isn't fair to expect a toddler to wait his turn to ride a bike or play with a truck. At around 18 months, allowing each twin to have his own toys cuts down on competition and fights. Every child likes to have something that she can claim as her property.

TOILET TRAINING

Toilet training, one of the most sensitive areas of your twins' development, should be a pleasurable experience for everyone. As your twins gain control over their own bodies, using the toilet is their first official indication that they are entering the "big kid" world. Teaching twins the magic of the potty is the same as teaching a singleton. And as any parent with older children will tell you, if you begin too early, the whole process will backfire, causing anxiety for your twins and frustration for you.

When to Begin Toilet Training

Children have physical control over their bladder muscles anywhere from 18 months to 3 years, with 2½ years as the average. If you consistently find your twins with dry diapers in the morning or after a nap, or they don't urinate for several hours during the day, they're probably physically ready for the potty. But children must be mentally mature as well. If they begin to ask about the toilet and show an interest in using it, chances are they are ready to begin. While many twins are primed to train at the same time, many more are not; especially boy-girl twins, where the difference can be six months or longer.

Separately or Together?

Training your twins separately, some parents find, is less confusing, with fewer accidents to deal with, but it takes longer. Therefore, most parents wait until both twins show readiness signs and train their twins together. If one twin is ready to train before the other, parents wait for the unready twin to catch up.

Training twins together has many benefits:

- When one twin walks off to use the potty, the other usually follows.

- Competitive twins (often identical boys) usually learn more quickly than the average child.

- The overall process takes less time than training them separately.

- Same-sex twins learn from each other through imitation.

Tips for Successful Toilet Training

- From an early age, allow your twins to watch you or an older sibling use the toilet—kids love to imitate.

- Take twins to the potty every two hours and make the experience pleasurable by having toys and picture books nearby. Never let them stay on their potty chairs for longer than 15 minutes at a time.

- Never push children into toilet training before they are ready, or encourage competition with unkind reprimands like "Why can't you use the toilet like your brother?"

- Incentives like colorful stickers and high-spirited praise work well, but keep them to a minimum if one twin is having difficulty getting the hang of it and becomes sensitive.

- Keep clothing simple during the process so twins can undress quickly and easily before using the toilet.

- Have realistic expectations—accidents will happen.

- If you can't decide what to buy—one or two potty chairs, or a seat that fits directly over the toilet—parents recommend two potty chairs for younger recruits (they can keep each other company), or one seat to share for older trainees.

In Sickness and in Health

It shouldn't come as a big surprise that when one twin gets sick, her sister is soon to follow. That means that even a simple cold could be stretched out for weeks as both children recover. It's useless (not to mention close to impossible) to isolate twins from each other, as most childhood illnesses are contagious at least 24 hours before any symptoms are exhibited. If your duo does get sick at the same time, simplify your life by forgoing their regular schedule. Let them tell you when it's nap time, dinner time, and bedtime. Simplify your household chores, too. When your kids are well, then you can pull out the vacuum. Until then, spend your time nursing your little ones back to health.

While caring for two sick infants or toddlers at once is very stressful, tending to one patient while his healthy brother stands by can take its toll on you, too. The well child often loudly exhibits his frustration with the situation, simply because he doesn't understand why his twin is getting all the attention while he is getting none. Allowing the healthy child to have a part in the caretaking of his ill brother can help to alleviate much of the whining. Simple tasks like delivering lunch or retrieving an additional blanket go a long way toward helping him feel needed and important.

Although illnesses are a major part of growing up, there are ways to keeping everyone healthier, cutting down on the severity of the illness.

- Encourage handwashing before and after eating, after using the toilet, and after your child blows her nose.

- Assign everyone in the household his or her own toothbrush, washcloth, and hand and bath towels, and discourage sharing. Use paper towels instead of cloth in the kitchen.

- Wash toys regularly with warm soapy water, especially if the kids love to put them in their mouths. Clean high-traffic areas like stair railings, telephones, and countertops with antibacterial soap.

- Keep kids healthy by making sure everyone gets enough rest and eats a balanced diet.

One More Pair?

The toddler years are a time of contradictions. On the one hand, double-trouble, however tired that expression has become, aptly describes preschool twins. From the moment they learn the words "no" and "mine," they'll test your patience on a daily basis. Yet it's also a delightful period. As your twins' special friendship with each other grows and they become active participants in the family, you'll find yourself secretly wishing for an additional set.

•8•

School Days

My parents should have separated Yvette and me more. They should have encouraged us to have different friends. Wherever I went, she had to go. Wherever she went, I had to go. But I often felt like I wanted to go by myself. But they'd say to me, "Take your sister, too." I didn't appreciate that. Sometimes I wanted to be away from her. I wanted to be with people who had invited just me.

Developmental Milestones

When they were infants, your twins made enormous strides both physically and mentally. As if by magic, they transformed right before your eyes, adding a new word or motor skill daily. Now that they've reached their school years, their developmental milestones are less pronounced, but continue to be important nonetheless. It's during ages 5 to 7 that children, especially twins, learn about their world outside their home as they spend more hours away from their parents and each other.

Enrolling in kindergarten is the high point for any 5-year-old child. The beginning of school means he's growing up, developing more independence, making new friends, and—possibly for the first time—parting company with his twin. Five-year-olds still enjoy alone time where they can set the rules of the game, but they're learning more about cooperation and can easily interact with a group of children. Most twins have an easier time socializing within a peer group. After all, they are masters at cooperation and taking turns. It's a talent they had to learn straight from the womb. They work well together solving puzzles and playing board games. Cooperation begins at home, though, where many twins help each other dress in the morning, patiently taking turns with clumsy buttons and snaps.

Morality comes into play at this age, too, as your twins begin to understand the difference between right and wrong. Yet sometimes they might take things a little too far. Many doppelgängers will "take the fall" for their twin—a sensitive sibling will often confess to a crime she didn't commit just so her counterpart won't be punished.

As their sixth birthday approaches, your twins are focused more on their new friendships and dealing with outside relationships than with family. They look more to their friends to answer their questions than to Mom and Dad. Opinions matter. And while peer pressure may not seem like an ideal way for any child to learn about life, relax. Children who imitate are simply learning to live in a larger society, trying to understand their position in life and how they fit into the big scheme of things. Feeling that they belong to a group actually helps them build self-esteem. Yet sometimes fragile twin egos get bruised at this age, especially if an independent twin has the need to break away from his more dependent sibling.

By age 7, children are ready for household chores as they take pleasure in completing a task. Their attention span has lengthened to a point where they actually will finish the project at hand. But give twins separate chores to complete—it cuts down on intertwin fighting and helps them to develop their own individuality. Physically, watch your twins' balance take hold as they learn to ride a bike. And it's also about this time that your kids will lose their very first baby tooth—a big milestone indeed.

Class Conscious: Should You Put Both Children in the Same Classroom?

In the 11th grade, the school district was forced to put us in the same class due to the amount of students. It was strange. Rob and I were always trying to outdo each other both academically and as class clowns. If there was a way to answer a question about Beowulf and insult our twin at the same time, we would do it.

The most important twin-specific issue facing parents of multiples at this age involves enrolling their duo in school. Should parents put their twins in the same class, or should they separate them? If your particular school district has a strict policy against putting siblings together and you decide not to contest the rule, then the decision has already been made for you. But other districts have no such policy and let the parents judge which is best for their particular family. If you find yourself in the latter situation, consider these compelling arguments on each side before deciding.

Advantages of Placing Both in the Same Class

- Twins usually adjust to school life more quickly when placed in the same class. Parents say this is a tremendous help if one twin is painfully shy. And for twins who have been inseparable for the last five years, it seems extremely harsh to abruptly divide the pair.

In the grade school where I was principal, we had parents who wanted their kids together. I remember a boy and girl who were not twins but were around 9 or 10 months apart. The boy was younger and dependent on his older sister, and the mother wanted them together in the same class. They did well together because they supported each other. I didn't think it was such a good idea at first, but in that particular case, the mother was right—the boy needed his sister's support and he was better off being in the same classroom with her.

- Twins have an instant friend and lunch buddy.

- Once the initial adjustment period is over, twins won't spend much time together, but they take comfort in knowing that they are in the same room.

They seem to like knowing the other one is in the same class. They each play with other children, but they periodically come back to each other throughout the day and do an activity

*together. After awhile, they go off and play with other kids
again. Then they come back to each other. Back and forth.
They seem to do well together.*

- Some twins work well together, studying as a team.

- It's more convenient. If there are only two kindergarten sessions, one in the morning and one in the afternoon, many parents don't relish the thought of driving to school four times a day. Unless there's a problem that warrants separation, why bother?

ADVANTAGES OF PLACING BOTH IN SEPARATE CLASSES

*It just so happens that the school decided to have two
kindergarten sessions—one in the morning and one in the
afternoon. So I was home in the morning with one and home in
the afternoon with the other. It was the first time I ever got to
be alone with each one. At first I thought it wouldn't be good
because Brian and David didn't know how to be alone without
the other, but it was the best!*

- Competitive twins fare better in separate classes, where they are free to progress at their own pace.

*Bruce and Gale started in a one-room country school where
they went to kindergarten together. With both of them being
such good students, it would not have been a problem if they
had remained in the same class for several grades. But at that
time, Verna and I didn't know how talented they might be. We
didn't want one to be a better student than the other and to
have comparisons made by the teacher or their classmates. So
we thought it would be better for them to have individual lives.
By being in separate classes, they could be by themselves like
most siblings are.*

- Twins having difficulty speaking also do better in separate classes, where they are forced to speak for themselves as well as have an opportunity to imitate the correct speech of others around them.

*I have a real problem. I believe they should be separated in
school. Even the preschool teachers have all recommended that*

they be separated because Conner always answers for Ryan. It's pretty bad. But my school district is so small, there's only one kindergarten class. I'm thinking about sending them to private school just so that I can separate them.

- Sometimes twins who are placed in the same class keep to themselves, rarely interacting with the other children, and subsequently have a more difficult time making new friends. In addition, "tough-guy" twins can band together and be disruptive.

- Identical twins who are often mistaken for the other benefit greatly when placed in separate classes, where teachers and students won't confuse or compare the pair.

How to Choose What's Best for You

While most parents choose to separate their twins for a variety of reasons, it's important to remember that no one knows your twins and their specific needs better than you. If you decide that your children would be better off in the same class, make your wishes known to your local school board. Just because your school system has made an arbitrary rule concerning sibling separation doesn't necessarily make it correct. The type of intertwin relationship should be the deciding factor, and every family should be judged individually. The ultimate goal of schooling (and parenting) is to raise an independent and socially responsible adult. How you get there should be your business. But remember, what may work one year for your twins may be totally wrong for them the following year. Therefore, be sure to reevaluate their needs at the end of each school year and adjust their future plans accordingly.

Although most of the school systems in this country have had sibling separation policies in place for decades, surprisingly no scientific evidence supports the rule. Another misconception is that all psychologists believe in the separation theory. It simply isn't so. Even Dr. Benjamin Spock in his book *Baby and Child Care* states (on page 760), "It seems foolish and cruel to have an arbitrary rule about separation of twins in school when there is no need."

If your children are to be in separate classes and up until this point haven't spent much time apart, it would be wise to slowly begin segregating them well before the first day of school. One way to begin the process is to run errands with just one child, leaving her sibling at home with another parent.

Top Five Birthday Party No-Nos

When twins are young, they hardly notice the coming and going of their birthdays. Once they reach school age, however, just like every other red-blooded kid, birthdays become important. So how do parents give each twin what she wants, short of planning two separate parties? As one mom solemnly noted, "They don't want to share much else, but they know that they have to share a birthday." With a little imagination, parents can pull off a successful party where each twin will feel special. But before you call Rent-a-Clown, consider these no-nos.

1. **One cake; one song.** Every child deserves to be in the birthday spotlight alone (even if it is only for a few minutes). Let each child choose her favorite cake (they don't have to be big; two small cakes will suffice) and then sing "Happy Birthday" twice—once for each child. But who gets sung to first? Alternate years, and don't worry—they'll remember whose turn it is.

2. **The shared gift faux pas.** By now, parents know that they should give each child her own special gift, but how do you delicately get the message out to well-meaning party guests who consistently show up with one toy for the twins to share? One mom handled this touchy situation by writing a poem and including it in each invitation:

    If you're thinking of a special gift,
    Let us help you with a clue.
    We like just about anything,
    Just as long as there are two!

3. **One guest list.** Insisting that your twins agree on the guest list is not only unfair but sure to start an argument. But how do you

avoid a crowd of children on the day of the party? First, decide on the guest count (it helps to make it an even number), then divide in half and allow each child to choose her own guests.

4. **Playing up twin status.** Presenting the "birthday twins" as a unit by dressing them alike on their special day erroneously reinforces to family and friends that the two are actually one. Encourage each child to choose his own special birthday outfit.

5. **Identical kids, identical gifts.** Many party guests, afraid to show favoritism, sometimes show up with two identical gifts. While not always a problem, especially for young twins, older twins may not appreciate the gesture. Once again, a simple note on the invitation can do the trick: "Jake's passion of the year: dinosaurs. Tom's passion of the year: airplanes."

Twins and Friends

As toddlers, twins are inseparable, always seeking out each other's company—but once school begins, it's inevitable that the pair will separate and experience unique events of their own. And separate friends should be a part of the mix. For some parents, this twin "breakup" can be sad, an end to toddlerhood. But it's important for children's developing self-esteem to form separate relationships. When twins play with "outsiders," it promotes proper speech development, boosts their confidence, and cultivates social skills that they'll need for the future. In effect, it readies them for the real world.

For close-knit twins, especially identicals, making new friends can be difficult. A twin may be reluctant to continue socializing with a new playmate who doesn't do things the way his twin does. And while a singleton is forced to make friends out of loneliness, twins are not—they have each other as playmates. Following your children's first birthday, encourage interactive play between your twins and their cousins, neighbors, or play group buddies. The longer you take to introduce your twins to other children, the more difficult the process of making new friends becomes.

When arranging play dates for older twins, it's wise to invite two friends over to play rather than one. If only one child is present, twins may either gang up on that child (and that's the end of that friendship!) or one twin may take her under his wing and exclude his twin. Having two playmates evens the playing field—each child can pick a buddy and break off into a smaller group as children often do.

As you nurture your twins' outside friendships, sooner or later one twin will be excluded when one receives an invitation that the other does not. How your left-out child reacts will depend greatly on how *you* react. It's unfair to think that if one twin is asked somewhere that the other twin should be included, too. If one twin gets invited to a birthday party and the other doesn't, for instance, make special plans to go to the zoo or park with the excluded sibling.

Tips to Encourage Outside Relationships

- Join a neighborhood play group and seek out same-aged playmates for twins early in their toddler years.

- Encourage (but never force) twins to make separate friends by allowing your children to invite playmates over after school or on Saturdays.

- If possible, enroll twins in separate preschool classes.

Twins Asserting Their Independence

My girls Rebecca and Susanna have their difficulties. They really want to be considered their own persons. It started around age 6 or 7. At first I thought it was partly due to Carlie, my other daughter, coming into the family, but then I realized it was school. They had been in kindergarten together but the school separated them in first grade. Once they started having their own experiences, they would come home and wouldn't want to share what they had learned in school. We're trying to get over that—letting them know that, yes, you are individuals. Mommy's not going to make a mistake of who you are. Don't fight so hard to be an individual.

*Nannette's getting ready to graduate, and Yvette still has
credits that she's lacking so she won't be able to graduate until
the end of the year. Nannette's loving the fact that she gets to
graduate by herself. She said, "Mom, do you realize that this is
the only thing other than getting married and having kids that
I'll get to do by myself?" The fact that she is doing this alone
makes her so happy. Yvette is just focused on finishing school.
She'll have her party next year. In the meantime, she's helping
out with Nannette's party and hasn't made any ill comments
about it.*

The need for twins to be different from one another by pulling
away from their special relationship is a natural step in growing up and
developing a sense of self. Some school-aged twins see their twinship
as an asset, others a liability. Psychologists say that intertwin fighting
is not only normal at this age, but needed in an effort for each child
to form his own individuality.

Twins have a doubly hard time in their quest to become individuals. As infants, all children see themselves as part of their caretaker, or
mother. But as they get older, they slowly understand their sense of self
and ultimately form their own identities. Twins, on the other hand,
must separate not only from their mother, but also from each other.
Compounding the situation is the twin bond itself—an intense relationship that exceeds the closeness of two different-aged siblings.
While twins want to individualize, they sometimes feel guilt at the
prospect of separating from their twin, someone they truly love.

For some twins, especially identical twins, the process of breaking
away is difficult. When similar-looking twins gaze into a mirror, whose
reflection do they see? Their own or their twins'? Are they one person
or two? Many young twins having trouble with identity formation
often use singular verbs when referring to themselves as a group: "I
went to the store with Mommy," or when asked their names, they
might answer using both, "My name is Kevin-Jeff."

While these problems eventually correct themselves, parents can
help their twins evolve their identities from an early age by following
these guidelines.

- Treat each twin as an individual by choosing different-sounding names and dressing each in different-style clothing.

- If possible, give each twin her own room, or at least her own space for toys and other possessions.

- When your twins are young, place a mirror inside each baby's crib. Point to her reflection often and repeat her name.

We were very cognizant of our desire to be individuals. Rob and I were always encouraged by our parents to be our own people. In fact, we both applied to Northwestern University, but he applied for early decision and I didn't. When I heard he got in, I actually withdrew my application. We wanted to go to separate colleges all the way.

The Need to Compare and Contrast Twins

It happens as early as day one while they're still in the hospital: Baby A weighs more than Baby B; Baby A is taller than Baby B. Parents naturally compare their new arrivals, looking for similarities as well as differences. Even if they never compared their other children of different ages, parents of twins now feel the need to distinguish one twin from the other. Solely because of their twinship, everyone—from family to strangers—compares one twin to the other and says things to twins that an adult would never think of saying to two siblings of different ages. "Which one of you is smarter?" is often a favorite.

While there is nothing inherently wrong with comparing twins (in fact, it's quite normal), constant contrasting of older twins often leads to intertwin competition. The pair will compete in school and sports, and even worse, they'll vie for parental attention. It can also lead to the appearance of favoritism when one twin's trait is praised, giving the impression of superiority over his counterpart. This can be damaging to fragile egos and self-esteem.

Identicals survive the compare/contrast dilemma a little easier since they begin on a level playing field—they're alike both physically and mentally—but fraternals, who are no more alike than any two siblings reared together, are unfairly compared. One will always be better at something than the other and they are often reminded of it on a consistent basis. Even parents who object to outsiders comparing their twins sometimes in their quest to instill individuality in their children do it too. "John is the athlete of the family while Susan is our straight-A student."

Top Five Ways to Avoid Unhealthy Competition Between Twins

While competition can help spur on many twins to achieve great goals, too much can hurt the twin bond and disrupt an otherwise harmonious family. Walking the fine line between spirited competition and unhealthy rivalry is shaky, but parents can help their twins to take off their boxing gloves by following these tips.

1. **Build on each child's individual strengths.** But don't be afraid to address weaknesses. "Yes, Mark's a better tennis player, but you're a great golfer."

2. **Reaffirm parental love.** From day one, twins are brought into a home where they must compete for attention. Remind your children often that there's plenty of love to go around. "Mom and Dad love both of you equally. You don't need to compete for our love. You already have it."

3. **All things are not created equal.** They may share a birthday, but twins need to realize that life is not 50-50, and someone will always be better at something.

4. **Don't fuel the fire.** Catch yourself when you inadvertently compare each child's abilities against the other's. Advise family and friends if they do the same.

5. **Avoid the firstborn rank.** Unless your family is part of British royalty, where the next in line for the throne will not be in dispute, don't refer to your twins as the younger or the older. Stressing birth order only intensifies twin rivalry.

THE PITFALLS OF LABELING

As soon as I introduced my twins to the world, the world immediately greeted each of my babies with a label: "Oh, you're the happy one, aren't you? And you, you're the shy one, right?" While these well-meaning people were merely trying to be friendly, their comments baffled me. How can they possibly make such a quick judgment, I thought. They don't even know my kids! Placing labels on twins is a common practice as family, friends, and even strangers struggle to differentiate one twin from the other. While comparing is natural, labeling is dangerous, inhibiting the growth and development of twins.

When parents classify each child daily with comments like, "Joan's the musical one, and Tom's the bookworm," twins hear them, internalize them, and soon believe them. In effect, Mom and Dad have branded them. Through a self-fulfilling prophecy, it becomes a part of them ("Well, if they said it, it must be true. I'm not the musical one, Joan is.") The result of these innocent comments is that children sometimes don't reach their full potential. If a child thinks that his twin has an edge on a specific talent, that child may step back and never try to achieve greatness in the same area. Comparing is normal, but labeling is too rigid and doesn't permit change. It inhibits development.

PLAYING FAVORITES

At different times, they get to me in different ways.
Momentarily, one becomes my favorite.

Although they hate to admit it, many parents do have favorites when it comes to their twins—it just depends on the day of the week.

Why It Happens

It's human nature to feel closer to one child than another. Unlike animals, humans bond with one offspring at a time. And when two infants suddenly appear in the picture, parents feel guilty when they don't have similar feelings for both. Favoritism can begin as far back as the day they are born. Parents of newborn twins, fresh from the hospital, report feeling closer to the more responsive twin, or the less fussy of the two, or in the case of premature twins, the one who is released from the hospital first, or the sicker twin still recovering in NICU and in need of more attention. But these are only temporary feelings, they say, and within weeks, their love for both deepens.

But what if they're not temporary feelings? What if your feelings for one twin never catch up and you find yourself drawn to one baby more than the other? All children have distinct temperaments and different rates of development. Some children are more difficult to be around; it's only natural to find yourself not wanting to be in his company.

Tips on Overcoming Favoritism

- Admit to yourself that you have a favorite and acknowledge that it's a normal feeling.

- Help the unfavored child deal with his unfavorable behavior. For instance, give the whiner an alternative way to ask for what he wants.

My mother and father spend a lot of time with me and my twin sons. Once they said to me that they think I have a favorite child. And so I asked them, "Well, who?" Then my father said, "That's the problem. Your mother thinks that you favor Conner and I think you favor Ryan." They're so funny. They think I have a favorite kid, but they can't agree on who I favor.

But That's Not Fair!

Just recently I had to buy David a pair of black pants and a belt for the school band. And Brian has now reminded me five or six times, "Well, you got David those black pants." Their sister Lindsay has more clothes than they do because she's a girl and she cares more, but they don't look at her wardrobe and say, "She has three pairs of tennis shoes and we only have one." They don't do that. They only compare what they have with each other. I could never go out and buy one of them a pair of tennis shoes and not the other. I make them both need things at the same time. If one of them is getting a new pair of blue jeans, they'd better both be getting a pair of new jeans.

This double-duty mom takes the "both or neither" approach when dealing with issues of fairness. Families admit it prevents feuding and bad feelings between twins, but it's a costly solution. Many parents give each twin the exact same item out of guilt or fear that they will show favoritism. And it doesn't take long for twins to pick up on this, manipulating the situation to their advantage. Children whose parents take this approach keep a mental tally of who got what when and remind parents on a daily basis. They learn early on that Mom or Dad can be coerced into giving.

With twins, it's easy to become overly concerned with trying to be fair, but like all things in life, nothing is ever 50-50. Moreover, trying to keep things equal all the time is an impossible task. What if one child needs money for college and the other has received a scholarship? Will you feel compelled to give the scholar the same amount of money as the child in need just to be fair?

From early childhood, concern yourself with giving each child what she needs by responding to her individually. Give because of need or love, not because of appeasement or guilt.

Twins as Adolescents and Adults

As parents watch their twins grow, they often worry about the intertwin relationship more than they would about the connection between any two siblings. Are the twins too dependent on each other, they ask? Are they too distant with nothing in common? How twins relate to each other as adults largely depends on how they weather that enchanting period of one's life called adolescence. When twins teeter precariously between childhood and adulthood, intertwin rivalry and jealousy is at its peak as the two fight for their independence.

The teen years cause the greatest stress on the family with twins. With peer pressure and the need to explore and experiment, not only do the pair break away from parental control, but they often deny their twinship as well. It can become even more disruptive if one twin matures faster both physically and emotionally than the other. Resentment may build if, for instance, parents feel one twin is more mature and ready to date while the other isn't. Do parents deny both twins the privilege when they wouldn't if the mature child were a singleton? A private, heart-to-heart talk with the less mature teen explaining that their decision to deny him the liberty to date is only temporary will help hurt feelings mend more quickly.

Older children still need boundaries, and parents need to set limits and be consistent in their enforcement. If the teens help to formulate the house rules, however, they are less likely to break them.

The need for privacy also increases during this period. Many same-sex teenage twins are relentless in their quest for their own rooms. Parents who aren't able to accommodate their children's insistent wishes can increase privacy by adding a room divider to the twins' bedroom, or offering each a separate closet or dresser. You might want to remind them that learning to share a room successfully is a good lesson since much of adult life is spent sharing.

While many twins may temporarily deny their twinship during adolescence, others become closer, taking solace in their bond. They might feel that no one understands them better than their twin. Unfortunately, they can unite together against their parents, fanning the generation-gap flames.

Whether your twins become inseparable buddies or mortal enemies, as any parent with grown children will tell you, during the teen years you're in for a bumpy ride. Don't forget to fasten your seatbelts.

By the time they reach adulthood, most twins who have adamantly denied their twinship usually rekindle their relationship. Not only is adolescence a marker for the type of relationship that they'll have as adults, twin type plays an important role as well. Identical females usually remain the closest out of all twin types followed by identical males. This is not surprising since most identicals are closer during childhood and share many of the same interests (not to mention DNA). Fraternal females are often closer than most singleton sisters, as are fraternal males, but much depends on how close they live to each other. While adult male-female twins are the least close of twin pairs, they are usually more connected than most male-female siblings, but their bond is due in large part on the effort (or lack thereof) of the female twin.

The Last Word

Who would have ever thought that having twins would be so complicated? Well, actually it isn't. Your mind may be reeling from all the information that you've just ingested, but relax—you already know plenty about parenting twins. Just follow your heart, and indulge me one last time with a few favorite clichés.

This Too Shall Pass

Whether it's from lack of sleep or just trying to adjust to your new life, the first year with new twins is definitely the hardest. But before you know it, your twins will be running around the house and you'll be missing the days when they were portable infants and you could hug them whenever you wanted (now you have to try to catch them first!). With this in mind, remember: When they start to throw the cat food around your kitchen, breathe deeply and repeat, "This too shall pass."

The Grass Is Always Greener on the Other Side of the Fence

With twins, there's never enough time to give each child that special one-on-one time. As you look at other parents cooing over their only child, it's easy to sigh to yourself and feel slightly envious. I have felt that way, and on those occasions when I have wondered about a different life, the feeling doesn't last long. My boys pull me back to my reality with their devilish smiles and wet kisses, and I think to myself that I must have done something extraordinary in a past life to have been so blessed.

Go with Your Gut

In this book, I've tried to give you various perspectives on the unique problems parents face raising twins—dress them alike, don't dress them alike; separate them for the day, don't separate them; put them in the same class, don't put them in the same class; and so on. But all these decisions can be confusing, not to mention overwhelming, for new parents. Am I doing the right thing, you ask? Will I hurt my children's self-esteem if I choose one way over another? While I encourage you to use this book as a guide, it's more important to listen to your heart and do what you think is best for your twins. Only you know what each of your children needs. Trust your instincts. They won't steer you wrong.

Appendix

Suggested Readings

TWIN SPECIFIC

The Care of Twin Children (2nd ed., rev.), by Rosemary Theroux and Josephine Tingley; Chicago: Center for Study of Multiple Gestation, 1984.

Gemini: The Psychology and Phenomena of Twins (2nd ed.), by Judy W. Hagedorn and Janet W. Kizzian; Chicago: Center for Study of Multiple Gestation, 1983.

Having Twins, (2nd ed., rev.), by Elizabeth Noble; Boston: Houghton-Mifflin, 1991.

The Joy of Twins, by Pamela Novotny; New York: Crown, 1988.

Keys to Parenting Twins, by Karen Kerkhoff Gromada and Mary C. Hurlburt; New York: Barron's, 1992.

Make Room for Twins, by Terry Pink Alexander; New York: Bantam, 1987.

Mothering Twins, by Linda Albi, Deborah Johnson, Debra Catlin, Donna Florien Duerloo, and Sheryll Greatwood; New York: Fireside, 1993.

Multiple Blessings, by Betty Rothbart; New York: Hearst Books, 1994.

The Parents' Guide to Raising Twins, by Elizabeth Friedrich and Cherry Rowland; New York: St. Martin's Griffin, 1984.

Twins and Supertwins, by Amram Scheinfeld; Baltimore: Penguin Books, 1973.

Twins: From Conception to Five Years, by Avril Clegg and Anne Woollett; New York: Van Nostrand Reinholdt, 1991.

Pregnancy and Prenatal Care

The Complete Book of Breastfeeding, by Marvin Eiger and Sally Wendkos Olds; New York: Bantam, 1987.

Nutrition for a Healthy Pregnancy: The Complete Guide to Eating Before, During, and After Your Pregnancy, by Elizabeth Somer; New York: Henry Holt and Company, 1995.

Pregnancy Bedrest: A Guide for the Pregnant Woman and Her Family, by Susan Johnston and Deborah Kraut; New York: Holt, 1990.

The Premature Baby Book: A Parent's Guide to Coping and Caring in the First Years, by Helen Harrison; New York: St. Martin's Press, 1983.

Vegetarian Pregnancy, by Sharon Yntema; Ithaca, New York: McBooks Press, 1994.

What Every Pregnant Woman Should Know: The Truth About Diet and Drugs in Pregnancy, by Tom Brewer and Gail Sforza Brewer; Baltimore: Penguin Books, 1988.

What to Eat When You're Expecting, by Arlene Eisenberg, Heidi E. Murkoff, and Sandee E. Hathaway; New York: Workman Publishing, 1986.

What to Expect When You're Expecting, by Arlene Eisenberg, Heidi E. Murkoff, and Sandee E. Hathaway; New York: Workman Publishing, 1986.

When Pregnancy Isn't Perfect: A Layperson's Guide to Complications in Pregnancy, by Laurie Rich; New York: Penguin Books, 1993.

The Womanly Art of Breastfeeding, by La Leche League International; 1993.

CHILD CARE AND PARENTING

The Baby Book, by William Sears, MD, and Martha Sears, RN; Boston: Little, Brown, 1993.

Dr. Spock's Baby and Child Care (6th ed., rev.), by Benjamin Spock and Michael B. Rothenberg; New York: Pocket Books, 1992.

New Mother Syndrome, by Carol Dix; New York: Doubleday, 1985.

Solve Your Child's Sleep Problems, by Richard Ferber, MD; New York: Simon & Schuster, 1985.

Touchpoints: The Essential Reference, by T. Berry Brazelton, MD; Reading, MA: Addison-Wesley, 1992.

Your Baby and Child: From Birth to Age Five, by Penelope Leach; New York: Knopf, 1989.

PERIODICALS

American Baby, 475 Park Avenue South, New York, NY 10016

Double Talk, P.O. Box 412, Amelia, OH 45102

Parenting, 501 Second Street, San Francisco, CA 94017

Parents, 685 Third Avenue, New York, NY 10017

Today's Father, National Center for Fathering, 10200 W. 75th Street, Suite 267, Shawnee Mission, KS 66204, (800) 593-3237

Triplet Connection, P.O. Box 997, Stockton, CA 95209

Twins Magazine, 5350 S. Roslyn Street, Suite 400, Englewood, CO 80111, (800) 328-3211

Twins' World Magazine, 11220 St. Joe's Road, Fort Wayne, IN 46835-9737, (219) 627-5414

Working Mother, 230 Park Avenue, New York, NY 10169

Resources

At-Home DAD
61 Brightwood Avenue
North Andover, MA 01845
(508) 685-7931
E-mail: athomedad@aol.com

Center for Study of Multiple Birth
333 E. Superior Street
Suite 464
Chicago, IL 60611
(312) 266-9093

Fathers' Resource Center
430 Oak Grove Street
Suite B3
Minneapolis, MN 55403
(612) 874-1509

International Cesarean Awareness Network
1304 Kingsdale Avenue
Redondo Beach, CA 90278
(310) 542-6400

La Leche League International, Inc.
P.O. Box 1209
Franklin Park, IL 60131-8209
(630) 455-7730

National Organization of Mothers of Twins Clubs
P.O. Box 23188
Albuquerque, NM 87192
(505) 275-0955

Parents of Premature and High Risk Infants International, Inc.
c/o The National Self-Help Clearinghouse
25 West 43rd Street
Room 620
New York, NY 10036
(212) 642-2944

Pregnancy and Infant Loss Center
1421 E. Wayzata Boulevard
Wayzata, MN 55391
(612) 473-9372

Twinless Twins Support Group International
Dr. Raymond W. Brandt, Ph.D.
11220 St. Joe Road
Fort Wayne, IN 46835-9737
(219) 627-5414

TWINLINE
P.O. Box 10066
Berkeley, CA 94709
(510) 524-0863

Twin Equipment

Four Dee Products
Department TW
6014 Lattimer
Houston, TX 77035
(800) 256-2594
Free catalog offers a variety of twin products, including the Nurse
Mate pillow (for help in tandem nursing), Double Bouncer seat,
and Connect Two (connects two single strollers to form a
double).

Mainly Multiples
21811 Constancia
Mission Viejo, CA 92692
(800) 388-TWIN
Fax: (714) 581-4008
Offers a variety of products for twins and triplets including newborn layettes (including preemie sizes), birth announcements, crib cocoon (crib divider), and twin scheduling pads.

Tot Tenders, Inc.
P.O. Box 998
Poway, CA 92074
(800) 634-6870
Makers of the Gemini Baby Carrier for Twins (double snugly sack).

One Step Ahead
P.O. Box 517
Lake Bluff, IL 60044
(800) 274-8440
General baby equipment and pregnancy supply catalog with some twin-specific items.

The Right Start
5334 Sterling Center Drive
West Lake Village, CA 91361
(800) LITTLE-1
General baby equipment and pregnancy supply catalog with some twin-specific items.

Nene
5651 E. Washington Boulevard
Commerce, CA 90040
(888) TWIN-001
Makers of the Double Delight twin crib (comes with baby bedding). Brochure available.

Twosomes, Inc.
35 Geneva Boulevard
Burnsville, MN 55306
(612) 898-3505
Coordinating twin apparel. Catalog available.

More Than One
1727-8A Sardis Road North
Suite 276
Charlotte, NC 28270
(888) 889-9109
Products designed for the family expecting multiples, including
strollers and Nene crib. Catalog available.

Twin Pleasures
(800) TWIN-BKS
Call to receive newsletter and catalog offering twin products and
books.

Free Samples of Baby Products

Ross Laboratories
Welcome Addition Club
(800) 222-9546
Receive a free case of Similac/Isomil infant formula as well as
monthly coupons and newsletter.

Gerber Products Co.
Gerber Baby Club
445 State Street
Fremont, MI 49413
(800) 443-7237
Receive coupons for infant formula (babies must be between
0 and 2 months old).

Carnation
(800) 242-5200
Receive a free 10-month subscription to *Very Best* magazine as well as coupons for Good Start Infant Formula, Follow-Up Formula, and Follow-Up Soy, and samples of other products and coupons.

Beechnut Nutrition Corporation
Multiple Birth Program
P.O. Box 618
St. Louis, MO 63188
(800) 523-6633
Call or write to receive a twins promotional packet of coupons for baby food, as well as information on label-saving promotions.

Evenflo Products
Consumer Relations
1801 Commerce Drive
Piqua, OH 45356
(800) 356-2229
To receive a twin starter kit, send a copy of your children's birth certificates.

Procter and Gamble
Consumer Relations
P.O. Box 599
Cincinnati, OH 45201
(800) 374-5887
Call to be placed on a mailing list to receive disposable diaper coupons and sample products.

Preemie Pampers
(800) 543-4932
Call to buy Preemie Pampers by the case.

Johnson & Johnson
Consumer Product Division
199 Grandview Road
Skillman, NJ 08558
(800) 526-3967
Call to hear about new products as well as free promotions. In addition, sign up for free twins gift packet.

Kimberly Clark Corporation
Consumer Service Division
2100 Winchester Road
Neenah, WI 54956
(800) 544-1847
Call or write for coupons for promotional items.

Index